Happy to Do It

GET YOUR 'SNAP' ON!

D1367650

RANDY DRAPER

ENDORSEMENTS

"Randy Draper is a very special person and his book, *Happy to Do It,* is also a very special read. I believe in this title 100% and live my life by it. This is a 'must read' for anyone, any age, any career stage, who wants to be inspired to be a better person and to take their level of service to new heights, both personally and professionally"

– **Tony Jeary** - *Coach to the World's Top CEOs and High Achievers*

"*Happy to Do It* is a great title for a book that opens the door to 'service with a smile' – something we all need to be offering! Randy's book is easy and enjoyable reading, and he offers realistic, do-able how-to's to help you get started."

– **Tom Ziglar** - *Proud Son of Zig Ziglar, Author and Motivational Teacher*

"Fortunately (or unfortunately depending on how you look at it), I get a lot of motivational type of books sent to me for review because of my place in the professional speaking industry. Many of the books are good and offer a good deal of insight, but oftentimes lack substance and are, quite honestly, boring. BUT... Randy Draper's new book, *Happy to Do It,* is the exception! Without a doubt, this book will touch your heart, encourage you beyond belief, and move you to action! I couldn't put it down. I've read it and reread it several times and get new insights and ideas in each reading. Disclaimer: I have to be honest and tell you that I'm a Randy Draper fan! Randy and I have been close family friends since junior high school and were college roommates. He is one of those special friends that even though years may go by without seeing each other, our relationship always stays the same. Randy is one of the few people who actually walks his talk and is the real deal when it comes to putting other people first, having a great attitude (no matter what!), and is blessed with a servant's heart. He and his wife Elizabeth are rich through and through! They love the Lord, love each other, are best friends, and have tons of friends who love and respect them. (Now that's cool!) They are true examples of what it means to be Christ-followers. Do whatever you have to do to get this book TODAY and get ready to be blessed!"

– **Robin Creasman** - *The Rockstar Speaker*
RockStarSpeaker.com

"I have often heard it said that attitude will determine your altitude. That being said, Randy Draper has done this old world good in writing his new book, *Happy to Do It*. He reminds us that attitude will indeed determine your outlook; and as a result, the outcome. Attitude is everything. Jesus taught it and we must embrace it. Read it and be blessed. You'll be recommending it to others."

– **Johnny Hunt** - *Senior Pastor - Woodstock Church*

"When it comes to life, we all face a choice—a choice of perspective. We can elect to look at it from a selfish, me-istic perspective. Or, we can choose to look at life from God's perspective and find ways to serve other people. Each choice leads down a very different path. In *Happy to Do It*, my good friend Randy Draper reminds us all of the power in choosing to look at life from a selfless, generous perspective. And through a myriad of personal experiences, he reveals the power, opportunities, and blessings that come with a life focused on serving others—a life that has an attitude of, 'Happy to Do It!'"

– **Ed Young** - *Senior Pastor, Fellowship Church*
Author, Outrageous, Contagious Joy

Happy to Do It
GET YOUR 'SNAP' ON!

RANDY DRAPER

HeartSpring Media
Published in conjunction
with Randy Draper
www.h2doit.com

First published by HeartSpring Media November 2010.

ISBN: 978-1-58695-052-1

This book is printed on acid-free paper.

Dedicated to
Andy and Joan Horner

Your love and friendship has
encouraged and inspired me.
You are an incredible example
of what serving others is all about.
You have enriched my life
and the lives of all who know you.
You truly are "Happy to Do It!"

ACKNOWLEDGEMENTS

I could never have finished this book without the love and encouragement of some amazing people in my life! I want to thank them individually.

Thanks to my wife, Elizabeth, who encouraged me to write this book and has motivated me every step of the way to get it finished. Her love and passion for God inspire me daily to be all that God wants me to be. She is my high school sweetheart and best friend on the planet. Elizabeth, I love you more today than yesterday, but not as much as tomorrow!

Thanks to my son, Kevin, who has harassed and encouraged me along the way! I appreciate your "Just Do It, Dad" attitude. You challenge me with your incredible ability to dream of the possibilities in life!

Thanks to my son, Kyle, and his wife, Lana. Your love for each other and the Lord are an inspiration to me. I cherish your love and encouragement!

Thanks to my parents, Jimmy and Carol Ann Draper, for the serving, loving and caring attitude that you have demonstrated in my life and the lives of countless people all over the world! You definitely have your "snap" on!

Dad, thanks for proofreading this book for me! Your words of encouragement helped me to stay focused and on task to see this become a reality!

Thanks to Dolly Crossley, the best mother-in-law I could have ever asked for! Thanks for proofreading the book and giving me your constructive criticism and encouragement. I love and appreciate you!

Thanks to my "pushy" editor, ghost writer and friend, Cheryll Duffie. You have been such an encouragement to me, helping me to stay on task and meet deadlines. Your sense of humor has lifted my spirits through the whole process and your editing skills have helped make this a much better book than if I had done it all by myself! I appreciate all the time and effort you put into making "Happy to Do It" a reality!

Thanks, Russell Lake, for putting your talent and creativity into making the cover and interior design of this book look fun and exciting! It communicates the passion and excitement that I have for this book and the anticipation that I want people to get when they pick it up off the shelf. You are a blessing to me!

Thanks to Brittani Prater, Jennifer Lake and Mary Stoldt for your help with the final proofreading. Your edits and suggestions made this the best book possible. I appreciate your attentiveness to the details.

I want to give an additional thanks to Andy and Joan Horner, founders of Premier Designs, Inc. You have shown me a genuine picture of the love of Christ for over 25 years. You have made an indelible imprint on my life, showing me what it looks like to be generous beyond imagination. You have challenged me to become a better leader, husband, father and friend! I love and appreciate you, and commit to continuing your legacy of serving, expecting nothing in return.

I am thankful for the Premier Designs family. I have learned a lot of the principles that I share in this book through all of the life experiences we have shared over these 25 years. I am so excited to see how God will use all of us to serve in the homes across America! It is a blessing to serve you and to serve with you! Thanks for loving and encouraging Elizabeth and me!

Finally, I want to give thanks to my Heavenly Father for giving me the thoughts and ideas that went into this book. You have inspired me, through your Holy Spirit, each step of the way. Thank you for using me to communicate your truths. Thank you for the gift of your son, Jesus. He makes the difference in my life! Thanks for teaching me to be "Happy to Do It", and for giving me daily opportunities to apply what I have learned into the lives of others!

FOREWARD

Over the years I have written the forewords for many books, but I have never had the opportunity to write a foreword for a book that excites me as much as this one. Perhaps it is because I know the author so well. In fact, I have known Randy Draper for over 50 years, and that is all of his life. I have watched him in every possible crisis and success one can imagine.

I remember the time his family uprooted him and moved him away from friends and from a position of incomparable success, with almost no time for him to prepare. He was elected president of his high school student body in Del City, Oklahoma at the end of his sophomore year. No sophomore had ever been elected student body president before. He attended "Boys State" that summer and was on his way to a great two year stint as president of his high school.

His father picked him up from "Boys State" and told him that they were moving to Dallas, Texas. With that move Randy went from being Mr. President, extremely popular and successful in the athletic teams at his high school, to being nobody in his new school in Dallas, an anonymous stranger in new surroundings.

It was hard on him, but he survived and thrived because he knew it was the right thing for his family to follow God's will to Dallas where his dad was to become the Associate Pastor for Dr. W. A. Criswell at

First Baptist Church in Dallas. It was a difficult move for him, but he soon found his new place to be one of enormous blessing and success because he was "Happy to Do It". It was there that he met the love of his life, Elizabeth. This was a love affair that would result in a lifetime of commitment as they married and built their family together.

Within a few years, they faced a financial crisis that would have destroyed most families. As a novice in the building business he found himself with debts he could not have imagined as the housing market crashed. He asked his dad about bankruptcy and his dad told him that it was a legal way to resolve insurmountable debt, but he should let God lead him in his decision whether or not to declare bankruptcy. On the way to the lawyer's office, God told him not to file for bankruptcy. He simply told his dad, "God wouldn't let me do it!" Randy obeyed and God was faithful.

He met with his creditors and promised to repay each one. Most were skeptical that he could do it, but agreed to let him try. It took him 10 1/2 years, but he paid back a debt of over two million dollars. His "Happy to Do It" attitude gave him the spirit, skill and means to keep his word and clear those debts.

He has been a leader in whatever he did wherever he has been. He and Elizabeth were one of the first couples in a new company called Premier Designs when it began 25 years ago. It started as a way just to make some extra money for the young family as they struggled with their financial challenges. Their hope was for it to generate some extra funds for food and house payment and other necessities.

It did that and more. Randy threw himself into helping Elizabeth with her "jewelry business." Together, they have made an incredible team. Elizabeth shares the same "Happy to Do It" attitude that Randy has and is a remarkable partner in business and ministry with him. Soon it became apparent that they faced a phenomenal opportunity with this young company.

They threw themselves into their fledgling business and God's blessings began to come faster and faster. Randy and Elizabeth learned during this time that they could not outgive God. Many times their tithes and offerings to their church cleaned out the last of their bank account, but God always came through with unexpected funds that more than made up what was given.

Together Randy and Elizabeth have demonstrated to the world that faith in God and a great "Happy to Do It" attitude with unceasing discipline and diligence can lead anyone to scale the obstacles they face. This book is about what God has worked out in Randy's life and in their family over these 25 years. God has gifted him to communicate effectively and skillfully with audiences all over the nation. Thousands of people today in Premier Designs have come into the company through Randy and Elizabeth.

Randy has passed on his "Happy to Do It" attitude to his entire family and to many whose lives he has touched. His older son is a youth minister and his younger son is involved in creative Christian ministries.

Randy is a born-again believer in the Lord Jesus Christ. He is a faithful churchman, and even has been widely used as a lay preacher. He is an ordained deacon and a faithful witness of the saving grace of God through the Lord Jesus Christ. He practices what he preaches. You cannot find a more optimistic and upbeat man than Randy. His life is a blessing to all who know him and he has honored God with his faith, his creativity, his energies, his talents and his life.

These pages will challenge you, bless and inspire you and cause you to want to excel in your work and to love the Lord Jesus Christ with all your heart. You will laugh and you will cry reading these pages. But mostly you will hear the voice of God speaking to you in a unique way through these messages. Enjoy what God has brought to you through Randy Draper.

Oh, yes, I know all these things are true because I am Randy's father! And no father could ever be prouder of a son than I am of Randy! Enjoy these pages, put these principles into your life and share these insights with your friends. Thanks for taking the time to read this significant work.

Jimmy Draper, November 2010

CONTENTS

INTRODUCTION

I learned much of what I am going to share with you in this book from helping a very special lady. My grandmother came to live with us when I was 9 years old. "Grandma" Lois Keeling Draper was crippled. She came down with polio at 10 months of age and one of her legs was about 4 inches shorter than the other one. I grew up helping Grandma get in and out of her bed, in and out of the house, in and out of cars, and anything else that she might need. I helped her put on her socks and shoes. I helped her up and down the stairs. You name it and I helped her! It was at times a burden, but it was much more than I could have ever dreamed. It was truly a blessing! It was an opportunity to serve a woman who had every reason in the world to complain, but always chose to see things from God's perspective and to view things positively! I learned from helping her all those years that my joy is not in what I have or don't have, but in the depth of my relationships. I found so much joy from helping and serving her, and I learned that helping others really does more for me than it will ever do for them.

I attended a men's conference over 25 years ago, and the guest speaker was a man by the name of David McGlaughlin. I do not remember much about him, but I will never forget the phrase he taught us that weekend. It changed my life! It changed my marriage. It made me a better son, father and friend. It was exactly what I had learned from helping Grandma all of those years! He taught us to be (snap your fingers) "Happy to Do It."

I loved it! It made so much sense to me! It became my life mantra! It is my response to every question. It is on my personal note cards. It is on my license plate. It is etched into my memory and will forever be on my lips! I have lived it and breathed it for most of my life and my life has been enriched far beyond my wildest dreams! I hope it will become your mantra too!

Anyone can be selfish and self-centered! It comes to us naturally. We are born that way! But the secret to living a life of purpose is realizing that God put us here to enrich the lives of others. He wants us to get out of ourselves and get into others! I know you are thinking, "If we are here for others, then what are they here for?" That, my friend, is just one of the questions that cannot be answered in *this* life.

Why are you here on this earth? I know, with God's help, that question can be answered. I believe one of the reasons I have had such a great and fulfilling life is that I learned a long time ago from my parents, Jimmy and Carol Ann, that the key to true happiness is serving others. Serving is the visible expression of "give and it shall be given to you" (Luke 6:38). And it really does work and makes an amazing difference in your life and the lives of others!

My wife, Elizabeth, and I have made it a practice to see who can out-serve the other. It has been our model for an incredible marriage for over 33 years!

I also learned 25 years ago that you can apply this serving lifestyle into your business as well. Andy Horner, founder of Premier Designs, Inc., has mentored me and has continually taught me that "You cannot do anything for someone else without it doing something for you too!" Elizabeth and I have built an awesome business by applying this God-inspired principle.

In this book I hope to encourage you to look past yourself, to see the people that God brings across your path each and every day as an opportunity. Be the love of Christ in their lives and serve them, expecting nothing in return! If you will learn to do that, you will be fulfilled beyond measure!

My goal in this book is to challenge and inspire you with the principles that I have learned through my life experiences. Whether you believe in the Bible or not, these principles will work if you apply them to your life and your business. I hope these principles will help you become all that God created you to be and will encourage you and inspire you to live your life "Happy to Do It"!

Get your 'snap' on,

Randy Draper

1

GET YOUR 'SNAP' ON!

Have you ever thought about the really important questions of life? You know, the ones you find yourself pondering in those rare moments of quiet reflection every decade or so.

Think about it ... If a man speaks in the forest and there's no woman to hear him, is he still wrong?

If a parsley farmer is sued, do they garnish his wages?

Do fish get cramps after eating?

What do little birdies see when they get knocked unconscious?

And my personal favorite—if love is blind, why is lingerie so popular?

Seriously, though, life presents lots of questions—real questions, tough questions. There are questions we already know the answers to, questions we don't *want* to know the answers to, questions that, if we look hard enough, we can find the answers to, and questions we'll never resolve this side of Heaven.

There is, however, one question that each of us must address on a daily basis. That question is, "Will you have an attitude of service today, or will this day be an 'all about me' day?" Every day, either consciously or otherwise, each of us is faced with the opportunity to either be "Happy to Do It" or "Hacked to Do It."

To bless others or be a burden.

To encourage or discourage.

To build up or tear down.

To … you get the idea. The bottom line is this: each day we are given the opportunity—no, the privilege and the responsibility—to have the attitude of Christ that God so desperately wants us to have toward others. It's an attitude that, in the best of times, can be challenging and in the worst of times, downright impossible—impossible, that is, except through the supernatural power of the Holy Spirit living within us. It is the spirit of living sacrificially for others that can be summed up in four simple words—*Happy to Do It!*

For you men, imagine you've just fought rush-hour traffic after a hard day at the office. You get the customary peck on the cheek from your wife only to be followed by a not-so-subtle "request" to take the trash out, and oh yeah, the dishwasher is leaking again. Think you could muster a genuine, "Happy to Do It" *without* the sarcastic tone?

For the ladies, picture yourself having just tucked in the last child for the night, the dishes are done, and the promise of a hot bath has kept you going the last two hours. Before you even begin running the bathwater, your beloved asks for a refill on his after-dinner tea or coffee. Can you honestly greet the "opportunity" to serve with an enthusiastic, "Happy to Do It"?

What about the boss who has put off the project details until the last minute and shows up in your office with a list of client-ordered changes *and* an 8:00 a.m. deadline tomorrow. So long, dinner with the family. Can you find it *anywhere* in yourself to respond, "Happy to Do It," without resentment creeping into your voice?

Isn't it enough in each of these circumstances to just fulfill the request? Can you really be expected to take out the trash, wait on someone, or work late with a "Happy to Do It" mind-set? If you're armed with the attitude of Christ, the answer is a resounding yes!

Not to put you on the proverbial guilt trip, but to many people you meet on a day-to-day basis, you're the best Christian they know. In fact, you may be the *only* genuine Christian they know. To them, you are the living, breathing embodiment of Christ here on earth. But like I said … no pressure!

Don't despair! Take heart and take comfort that this seemingly impossible attitude, this "Happy to Do It" perspective, can actually be developed. It's all a matter of conditioning. You can literally change your outlook from a "looking out for number one, what about me?" mind-set to one in which you automatically respond in a positive and Christ-like manner—say, for example, the "Happy to Do It," sacrificial manner of Christ!

Let me show you what I mean. Out loud, spell out the word *silk* five times. Say it with me:

S-I-L-K.

S-I-L-K.

S-I-L-K.

S-I-L-K.

S-I-L-K.

Now quick—what do cows drink? Did you say *milk?* Think again. Cows don't *drink* milk. They *make* milk and drink water.

But did you see how quickly you could be conditioned to say *milk?* The same is true with your attitude. With just a little conscious effort, you can begin to condition yourself to have a "Happy to Do It" attitude, first in the easy situations and eventually under more challenging circumstances. Before long, this "attitude of gratitude" will become your natural default. I like to snap my fingers when I say "Happy to Do It", because it mentally "snaps" me into this conditioned mindset. Not only will you serve with gladness, but you'll also soon get to the point

> **With just a little conscious effort, you can begin to condition yourself to have a "Happy to Do It" attitude, first in the easy situations and eventually under more challenging circumstances.**

7

where you don't even realize you're doing it! What's more, you'll actually begin to look for opportunities to live out Christ before others. Talk about the "sweet spot" of Christian living!

Let me share three insights from the Bible that I believe will help you begin to adopt a "Happy to Do It" attitude. These three principles are:

- Happiness is an inside job.
- Attitude is everything.
- If it is to be, it is up to me.

Let me explain how each of these principles has helped me to grow in my walk and witness for the Lord each and every day that I have put them into practice.

Happiness Is an *Inside* Job.

The first thing you have to realize is that happiness is an *inside* job. It can't be dependent upon people or things or circumstances. It's got to come from within.

A recent poll asked people what they needed to be happy in life. Although a few of the answers ranged from the bizarre to the boring, most of them centered on four common themes:

- They want to be loved.
- They want to make a difference in the world.
- They desire security.
- They want comfort.

The amazing thing is that *all* of these needs, hopes, and desires can be met through a relationship with Jesus Christ. The most famous of all Bible verses, John 3:16, says it so clearly, "For God so loved the world, that He gave His one and only Son, that whoever believes in Him shall not perish, but have eternal life." Look again at the four primary "wants" of most people and how this one verse, this one promise among thousands from our Heavenly Father, addresses *all* of these needs. It tells us that we're loved. It sets us apart from nonbelievers through the gift of Jesus Christ and as a result, sets us up for the unique opportunity to make a difference unlike anyone else in the world. It promises security through eternal life and provides the comfort that as believers, we shall never truly perish. Amazing, isn't it? The four biggest desires of an overwhelming majority of people can be met in one person—one person we invite to take up residence in our heart and soul—Jesus Christ. Like I said earlier, happiness is definitely an *inside* job.

> **The four biggest desires of an overwhelming majority of people can be met in one person—one person we invite to take up residence in our heart and soul—Jesus Christ.**

In contrast to what people list as the elements of happiness, Webster's Dictionary defines happiness as "a state of well-being and contentment."[1] While I'd never doubt "old man Webster's" knowledge, I'd have to say that I've known many, many people who seem to have all the makings of well-being, but the contentment part is just not coming through for them and as a result, they are anything but happy. Sure, they're living in spacious homes, driving new cars off the showroom floor, keeping up appearances in the hippest clothing, and hitting on all cylinders at their job. They've got well-being running out their ears. The catch, however, is that where there is no contentment, there is no happiness.

So while we find in Christ the only one Person who can bring us true *inside* happiness, God takes this happiness thing a step further by telling us in Proverbs 29:18c, "Happy is he who keeps the law" (NASB). Let me share with you the amazing extension of this verse, and that is,

---

1   Merriam-Webster. "happiness." Merriam-Webster On-Line. http://www. merriam-webster.com/dictionary/happiness (accessed October 9, 2009).

when you greet people with a "Happy to Do It" attitude, they frequently respond similarly.

I had this play out in my own life recently when I glanced in my rearview mirror and saw the flashing red and blue lights of a police car behind me. "Man, I wonder what poor guy he's going after," I said to Elizabeth. Several seconds later I noticed all the other cars on the road were hanging back and it was just me and the officer keeping pace.

"Looks like I'm about to finally get a ticket," I told Elizabeth, to which she unsympathetically replied, "Well, it's about time. You need one!"

As a bit of background about my colorful driving history, I should explain that for more than twenty years I've been stopped on a regular basis, but have yet to receive a ticket for speeding. It has become a longstanding family joke about how my "Happy to Do It" attitude has bailed me out of ticket after ticket, regardless of the circumstances.

I pulled to a stop and rolled my window down to the approaching officer. "Sir, could I see your license and proof of insurance?" he asked.

"Sure. Happy to Do It."

"Do you know what you were doing wrong?"

"I have no idea," I said.

"You were going sixty-two in a fifty-five," he explained.

"I am soooooo sorry," I told him honestly.

Before I finished my heartfelt apology, the address on my license had already caught his eye. "Colleyville? I got a good buddy who just joined the force over there. Can't say enough good about it. Say, I hear ..." and on and on he talked, striking up a one-sided conversation with me all because I greeted him with a "Happy to Do It" attitude—something you can be certain doesn't happen too often in his line of work.

It wasn't long before he quit extolling the virtues of my hometown and issued me nothing more than a simple verbal warning: "Mr. Draper, you really do need to slow down a bit."

"Yes, sir. Happy to Do It," I told him and was on my way. Funny thing is, dealing with the officer was the easy part. It was the chiding by my lovely lady and her claims of, "That's not fair!" that were the more challenging part of my latest tangle with the law. But like the responsible spiritual leader of my family that I am, I quickly told her, "Elizabeth, life is not fair. So just get happy!"

We're living in crazy and chaotic times. It seems like everyone is being sued or suing someone else. Modern-day America has become a litigious society, meaning that just about anyone can sue anyone else or a company for either a real or perceived wrongdoing. I can't help but believe that if folks would take to heart the words of God, again in Proverbs 29:18c, "Happy is he who keeps the law," we'd all be a lot closer to personal happiness.

Case in point, a Charlotte, North Carolina man insured his recent purchase of exclusive cigars against … are you ready for this? *Fire!* Within the first month of owning and insuring the cigars, he had smoked them all and subsequently filed a claim against their loss, stating that he had lost them all in a series of "small fires." When the insurance company refused to pay the claim, the man sued them and won the judgment. Rather than endure a costly and lengthy appeal, the insurance company accepted the judge's ruling and paid the man the $15,000 settlement. Within days of cashing his insurance check, the insurance company had the man arrested on twenty-four counts of arson—one for each fire he intentionally set to light each of his prized cigars.

You see, folks, it's not enough to just obey the literal law, but we must also honor the laws set forth by God, willingly submitting to His ways and not constantly seeking ways to escape through a loophole. With God's laws, it is the condition of the heart that is just as important as the action of the hands. To reach the goal of happiness, obedience and contentment have to go hand-in-hand.

The book of Psalms provides a wealth of advice for striking this delicate balance of obedience and contentment against the constant counter-pull of God's ultimate gift of trust—free will. Verse after verse in this Old Testament book offers guidelines for not just surviving, but thriving throughout this journey we call life. Among the pointers, the psalmist "suggests" repeatedly that the oh-so-simple path to happiness oftentimes comes down to who we hang out with (and frequently who we *don't* hang out with—namely, our Heavenly Father). Loosely translated, Psalm 1 tells us, a happy person does not get advice from the ungodly; he refuses to become a part of people who laugh at God; and he doesn't spend time with those who are habitually rebellious toward God. What he's saying here is that if you want to snag this thing called happiness, you might need to take a good long look at who you're spending your time with.

Think of your immediate circle of close friends—the first ones you'd call with good news or a serious need. Ask yourself these questions about them:

- Do they look at life from God's perspective?
- Do they strive to be all God wants them to be?
- Do they encourage *you* to be all God wants you to be?

If the answer to *any* of these questions is no, you need to give serious thought to how much time you spend in their company because, like it or not, they are having an influence on you.

Let me be clear to explain that I'm not saying *not* to ever associate with these people. The catch, however, is that *you* are the one who is supposed to be influencing *them*, not the other way around! So, be their friend. Be their encourager. Be an example. Just also be conscious of how much time you spend in their company and strive to make it as Christ-honoring as possible.

Not surprisingly, beyond paying special attention to who we spend our days with here on earth, God also commands us to make sure we commit an honorable amount of our days (or parts of our days) to learning and growing in our relationship with Him. Take a moment and meditate on these two verses:

Blessed are all who fear the LORD, who walk in His ways (Psalm 128:1).

Blessed are they who Keep His statutes and seek Him with all their heart (Psalm 119:2).

Seems simple enough, doesn't it? A cause-and-effect relationship reduced to its most simplistic form. Follow the Lord, get happiness. What could be easier? Nothing, if you spend your days polishing your halo and strumming your harp. For the rest of us, this simple formula tends to present a bit of a problem on a fairly regular basis.

Again, it's that sneaky free will that keeps creeping into the picture. It's the reason many of us have time to read the newspaper in the morning, but can't seem to squeeze in a quiet time for a moment of prayer. It's the reason we manage to have enough money to indulge many of our leisure activities, but don't give more in the offering plate. It's even the reason we're full of energy for Saturday night socializing, but can't manage to pull ourselves out of bed for church the next morning—even the *late* service!

It all comes back to who we spend time with and who we don't; how we spend our time—intentionally or otherwise; and how we condition ourselves to respond (again, intentionally or by default). Moms across the country have always been right regarding the impact of our friends: You are the company you keep. For believers, the directive is short and sweet: Get with God. Everything else is second.

Let's assume conviction is setting in and you've committed to improving your efforts toward Heavenly obedience. Good for you! You've taken note of areas where you can quickly increase your "obedience score" and are making conscious inroads toward improving your daily walk with the Lord. Now, remember the second half of the happiness equation we spoke of earlier.

Obedience + Contentment = *Happiness*

Contentment. If obedience is a challenge, I've got news for you— mastering contentment is not for the faint-hearted. If it was, why would the diet industry generate almost $50 billion dollars a year[2] in sales on machines, pills, and potions from millions of discontented people? Or why would your local bookstore have entire departments devoted to self-help books written by many self-appointed "life coaches"? That reminds me of the guy who went to his neighborhood bookstore looking for one of these books. When he couldn't locate the self-help section of the store, he asked a saleslady, "Ma'am, could you show me where the self-help section is?" Though quick-witted, she ultimately proved unhelpful when she replied, "Well, sir, if I told you where it was, that would defeat the whole purpose, wouldn't it?"

Could it really be that there are so few of us who are truly content with who and what we are that we spend personal fortunes trying to make ourselves look good on the outside when, in reality, all God wants is for us to look good on the *inside?*

> " **Your worth and value are in who you are, an individual made in the image of God, not in what you look like, where you live, and what you drive.** "

You see, it doesn't matter to God if your hair is falling out, your clothes are out-of-date, and you look like the "before" picture for a Slim-Fast commercial. To Him, you are of immeasurable value because you were created in His image. Your worth and value are in *who* you are, an individual made in the image of God, not in what you look like, where you live, and what you drive. Beyond this, if you've made the decision of a lifetime to claim Christ as your Savior, your value is in *whose* you are. The Bible tells us straight up that we belong to Christ

---

2   Bloomberg Businessweek. "The Diet Industry: A Big Fat Lie; Pro: A Pound of Trash." Bloomberg.com Business Exchange. http://www.businessweek.com/debateroom/ archives/2008/01/the_diet_indust.html (accessed September 1, 2009).

because we've been bought with a price. The price was Christ's blood at Calvary. Pretty hard to keep the "poor me" persona going when you take this into consideration, isn't it? After all, if God is content with who you are, shouldn't that take care of all the doubts and second guessing concerning your self-worth? Works for me.

If you're looking for an example of someone who had the contentment gig in perspective despite some most unfavorable circumstances, the apostle Paul is a stellar example. Chained and bound in a first-century jail, Paul penned these inspiring words:

> "For I have learned to be content whatever the circumstances. I know what it is to be in need, and I know what it is to have plenty. I have learned the secret of being content in any and every situation, whether well fed or hungry, whether living in plenty or in want. I can do everything through him who gives me strength" (Philippians 4:11–13).

What did Paul learn that he can teach us two thousand-plus years later? He learned that the key to happiness is an inside job and that it is available through the person of Jesus Christ. He also realized that his happiness wasn't based upon his surroundings or what he had or didn't have. It all came down to one thing—a relationship with Jesus Christ. Not the trappings of religion that bogged down even the people of his day, but a growing and ever-deepening relationship with the one and only Son of God.

In my experience, the obedience and contentment tango are just that—a dramatic dance of two characteristics that go counter to our natural inclinations of wanting what we want, when we want it, and how we want it—and then not being happy once we have it. However, when mastered, these two Christ-honoring traits can flow through us and bless others like little else in this crazy world. My advice when tackling these two hallmarks of basic Christian living are to begin by being obedient to the Lord's command to rely upon Him and applying the principles He lovingly provides in His word, the Bible. Take comfort in knowing that where there is genuine obedience to God's word, contentment will follow. That's a cause-and-effect relationship that you can take to the bank!

> " **Whoever you are, wherever you are, whatever your circumstances— attitude is everything!** "

Attitude Is Everything!

So now you're working the obedience and contentment challenge. The next principle that takes you closer to claiming the "Happy to Do It" perspective is understanding that whoever you are, wherever you are, whatever your circumstances—attitude is everything! Think I'm kidding? Learn from the two guys who found themselves as cellmates in a military prison. The first guy asked his cellmate, "What are you in for?"

"I'm in for thirty days," number two replied.

Curious about the lengthy sentence, the first guy asked, "What did you do?"

"I went AWOL," his partner answered. "What about you?"

"Hey, I'm only in for three days," he said.

"Three days?" asked the second guy. "What did you do?"

Hesitantly, the first guy replied, "I killed the general."

Unbelievingly, the second guy was immediately filled with injustice. His side trip into town for an unauthorized "night on the town" was seemingly costing him ten times the sentence of his upbeat roommate. He couldn't contain his indignant attitude and just had to know more. "Let me get this straight," he said. "I'm in here for thirty days just for going AWOL for a night, but you killed the general and you only got three days?"

"They're hanging me on Wednesday," his new buddy deadpanned.

A bit extreme to make my point? Definitely. But it's safe to say the condemned guy made a lasting impression on his AWOL friend, and that impression was to look for and find the good in every situation. Not to sound overly Pollyanna-like, but regardless of where you find yourself right now, there is a silver lining to be found, a blessing to be uncovered, and a positive perspective to take.

Whether it's a startling diagnosis, a personal betrayal, financial ruin, any other affliction of the human condition, believe it or not, there is good to be found. I'm not saying it's the preferable path to happiness, but sometimes it is the road the Lord would have us travel to arrive at where He sees fit for us to go. Twenty-plus years ago, Elizabeth and I lost more than two million dollars in the home construction business. For weeks at a time, failure and all the psychological and physiological symptoms it brings with it, was my constant companion. I had failed my family, my creditors, and my contractors. You name it, I was failing them. My days were filled with berating phone calls and table-banging face-to-face meetings with attorneys, suppliers, and bankers. They called me names. They questioned my business sense. They doubted my character. While these were undoubtedly some of the darkest days at the over-extended Draper household, they weren't without blessings and a perspective I'll forever be grateful for.

Chief amongst the lessons I learned throughout this rough patch is whatever the path, God wants His people to be positive people. You've got to remember that it's not just in the glory times that we're living for the Lord and being His agents here on earth. It is, in homage to the classic Clint Eastwood movie, in "the good, the bad, and the ugly" times that we are to be His positive examples to a lost world.

This not-so-easy, only-through-the-Holy-Spirit lifestyle all boils down to attitude.

Not moods.

Not feelings.

And certainly not circumstances.

Attitude … attitude … and yeah, more attitude.

One of the easiest ways I've found to "encourage" my attitude to be all that it should be is actually two-fold, and that is to *see* something positive in every situation and to *say* something positive to everyone I meet. Easy? Not so much. Worth it? Without a doubt!

I've even taken to naming this attitude of gratitude that helps me not just survive most days, but to thrive. I call it my "rejoice regardless attitude." Let me give you an example: Sign seen posted on the corner of a busy neighborhood intersection, "Lost dog—three legs, blind in one eye, missing right ear, tail broken, recently castrated. Answers to the name of 'Lucky.'" Now that's a canine with a can-do attitude!

Paul commands us in Philippians 4:4, "Rejoice in the Lord always. I will say it again: Rejoice!" Not once but twice does he tell us to rejoice.

> **This rejoicing mind-set has got to be the default, not the attitude of convenience.**

And *when* does he tell us to rejoice? When we've got enough money to cover all the bills? When the next "big deal" goes through? When he finally proposes (or she says yes)? Not so much. This rejoicing mind-set has got to be the default, not the attitude of convenience.

Paul was nothing if not persistent. In his characteristic passionate style of moving people to come to know the Lord, he elaborated on this rejoicing theme again in 1 Thessalonians 5:16–18 when he said, "Be joyful always; pray continually; give thanks in all circumstances for this is God's will for you in Christ Jesus." There it is again—that challenge to continually see the good whatever the situation, that "rejoice regardless" attitude I'm telling you about.

For me, these verses not only challenge me to remain positive when my flesh says it's easier to throw a pull-out-all-the-stops pity party, but they also answer that often-asked question about God's will for each of our lives. Look at 1 Thessalonians 5:16–18 again, this time in bullet form:

- Be joyful always (v. 16).
- Pray continually (v. 17).
- Give thanks in all circumstances (v. 18).

Why? "Because it is God's will for you in Christ Jesus" (v. 18). I'm thinking if you master these three directives, then your days would have to be off-the-charts terrific, one "joyfest" after another. Think about it. It's darn near impossible to be negative if you're staying busy giving thanks.

Take my "give thanks" challenge and see for yourself. Begin a list of things—*all* of the things you have to be thankful for. There's the obvious: family, friends, health, home, etc. But get beyond (and I mean *waaaaayyyy* beyond!) the immediate, automatic answers. Think of the obvious—oxygen, water, sunshine. Think of the necessary—toilet paper, electricity, toothbrushes. Think of the extras that make life pleasurable—Baby Ruth candy bars, pick-up basketball games, a terrific day fishing. I'm betting you won't be too far into your list before you're overcome with an incredible sense of thanksgiving. What's more, this attitude has a way of staying with you once you really take stock of all the countless blessings you have. A quick glance back at your list on the darkest of days can fend off approaching clouds of gloom and despair. Chances are you'll be re-inspired and will have thought of even more things to add to your list as your days go by.

This "rejoice regardless" attitude also works remarkably well as a sleep aid on those nights when you find yourself tossing and turning, replaying the "would haves" and "should haves" of the day through your mind. Remember the words from the Bing Crosby classic:

When I'm worried and I can't sleep,
I count my blessings instead of sheep,
and I fall asleep, counting my blessings.

Try it tonight. I absolutely guarantee you'll be sawing some Zzz's before you finish your list.

Along these lines, a closely related principle to the "rejoice regardless" attitude is the "worry-free" attitude. Not surprisingly, Paul has an opinion about tangling ourselves up with all the baggage of burdensome worry. In Philippians 4:6–7, he challenges us to adopt a "worry-free" attitude and to get to the *real* business of living as he says, "Don't fret or worry. Instead of worrying, pray. Let petitions and praises shape your worries into prayers, letting God know your concerns. Before you know it, a sense of God's wholeness, everything coming together for good, will come and settle you down. It's wonderful what happens when Christ displaces worry at the center of your life" (The Message).

Much like the happiness equation we discussed earlier, having a victorious attitude can be simplified into a basic equation:

Don't Worry + Instead Pray = Peace

Sadly, many, many of us—believers and nonbelievers alike—get it backward. We worry about *everything* and pray about *nothing.* It's no wonder we're frustrated, disappointed, and discouraged on a daily basis. It's like trying to do a math problem over and over but still getting the wrong answer. You've got to have the right factors to get the answer you're looking for. It's not rocket science; it's basic arithmetic.

Years ago, I was driving alone in my car across the Dallas/Ft. Worth Metroplex when I was overcome by feelings of hopelessness and a sinking self-worth. I think my subconscious must have been working overtime, compounding big challenges and obstacles and making them seem even bigger. When they finally got to the forefront of my thoughts, they had taken on full-blown, out-of-control, "I'll-never-get-out-of-this-alive" status. I was sinking fast, and I couldn't blame anyone but myself.

I had more bills than I could ever repay in a lifetime. I had attorneys from every direction chasing me, telling me how worthless I was, chewing me out, cursing me out, and threatening me. For all appearances, it was not good to be me at this particular point in my life. What's more, not only was I "in deep" to banks, suppliers, and individuals, in some whacked-out coping mode, I think I had even taken to almost enjoying living the "poor, pitiful me" persona.

Back on the interstate, the doom and gloom in the car was intensifying with every mile I traveled (think Pigpen from the *Peanuts* cartoon and his ever-present cloud of dirt and dust—except for me it was a dark, dark cloud hovering above my car and trailing me down the highway!).

Wallow.

Wallow a little bit more.

Wallow just a little bit more, for good measure.

"Pssssst. Hey Randy?" What was that?

"Randy. It's me, God. You're worrying again."

What could I say? When the Holy Spirit calls your bluff, there's pretty much no sense in trying to hide. No under-the-stairs crawlspace can hide you from the persistent, loving, convicting (did I mention persistent?) voice of the Holy Spirit when He's calling you out.

"Yeah, you got me. I'm worrying, all right," I answered.

"Randy, you're *worrying*," came the voice in my heart.

"I know, I know, God, but I can't help it. I'm *worried*," I feebly explained.

"Why don't you try praying?" He pressed me. (Talk about the mother of all rhetorical questions!). "Your value and worth are in *who* you are and in *whose* you are. Remember *that* and quit worrying."

"Okay, I'm with you, God. I'll do it," I answered and began to pray. And drive. And pray. And drive. All the way home.

You know what happened? No, my bills weren't miraculously paid. I wasn't suddenly welcomed back by former friends who had stopped finding me "acceptable company." And yes, I still kept receiving some less-than-uplifting phone calls. But just a few minutes into my prayers of desperation, the inside of my three-months-behind-on-my-note car became a sanctuary—a sanctuary of peace, filled with the comfort and the indescribable security of knowing that whatever the outside world thought of me or threw at me, I was of immeasurable value to the only person in all of Heaven and earth who truly mattered for eternity—Jesus.

From that point on, my tires seemed to be floating above the highway, unaffected by the potholes and rocks that cluttered the pavement. Come to think of it, that was pretty symbolic of where I found myself on that particular day. The "potholes" and "rocks'" of life were still coming at me (and would continue to do so), but despite the appearance of circumstances to the contrary, I knew the victory was mine.

So, apparently, did the guy who hired a professional worrier. Boasting to his buddy one day that he had finally gotten rid of all his worries, the friend anxiously wanted to know how his buddy had so quickly become carefree. "Yeah, it's a great deal," the first guy explained. "I just hired myself a professional worrier and suddenly, no more worries!"

Still curious for more details, the second friend pressed for the specifics of such a deal. "How much is that going to cost you?" he asked.

"Fifty thousand dollars," said the newly stress-free fellow.

"Fifty thousand dollars! You're already in debt up to your ears on everything from your house to your car to your credit cards. How are you *ever* going to pay that guy $50,000 to worry for you?"

"That's *his* problem," came the calm reply.

The irony of this story is that each of us has someone who came for the very purpose of relieving us of all our worries; the big ones, the little ones, the real ones, even the imagined ones. That person, quite naturally, is Jesus Christ. And while it won't cost you a dime, it cost Him His life—a life He voluntarily gave up for you and me. It seems to me that the least we can do is honor this unfathomable gift by handing over our worries and not making His death in vain.

Let me give you one more type of attitude to strive for in the lifelong quest for happiness: an attitude of service. Once again, in the book of Philippians, Paul tells us just what we need to make this possible. Philippians 2:5–7 says, "Your attitude should be the same as that of Christ Jesus: who, being in very nature God, made himself nothing, taking the very nature of a servant …" Earlier in the New Testament Jesus tells His disciples, "I am among you as one who serves" (Luke 22:27b). Think about these words from Jesus' perspective. He wasn't some down-on-His-luck, no-options-available-to-Him kind of guy. He was the King of kings, Lord of lords, Son of God, and yet, He came to redeem our corrupt and self-absorbed world and to meet our needs, including carrying the burden of worry for our cares and concerns. So humble was He that He insisted on washing the feet of His disciples to give them a tangible picture of what it meant to have an attitude of service.

Think of these three attitudes—the "rejoice regardless" attitude, the worry-free attitude, and the attitude of service—as a kind of trifecta of living like the Lord. Don't expect to wake up tomorrow and have them all mastered. It's a day-by-day thing, kind of like exercise. You didn't pack on those extra ten pounds overnight. Likewise, you can't drop them overnight. The same is true of gaining ground in this quest for Christlikeness. It's a gradual process with endless opportunities to learn from and serve in. Don't be discouraged if you stumble and old ways re-surface temporarily. Keep your eyes on the Lord and your heart before God and the attitudes will come in their right time.

If It Is to Be, It Is Up to Me.

That's a powerful statement for just ten little words.

It's twenty keystrokes that speak volumes.

Do you catch what it's telling you? This hunt for happiness rests squarely on your shoulders. Yes,

> **Develop a healthy perspective of life.**

it's an "inside job" that is most completely manifested in a relationship with Jesus Christ. And yes, your attitude can be a deal-breaker in whether or not you get to the point of experiencing true happiness regardless of your circumstances. But paramount to both of these principles is that no one can "do" happiness for you. You can't put it off on anyone else to make it happen for you—not your spouse, your kids, your friends, or your co-workers.

One of the best ways I've found to work toward happiness is to develop a healthy perspective of life. It's okay to admit that it's *work* living for Christ. It's *work* being all God wants you to be. It takes commitment and perseverance. It's certainly not for the weak of spirit. My dad pastored churches for over thirty years and had one saying that did a great job of summing up the Christian walk: "Being a Christian isn't a way of doing certain things; it's a certain way of doing everything."

Another way I've found to make a bit of progress on the happiness hunt is to take one Scripture at a time and apply it whenever and wherever you can in your daily life. Commit to living that Scripture out at every available opportunity and it won't be long before you'll have the chance to make good on your word to "be the word."

> "**Being a Christian isn't a way of doing certain things; it's a certain way of doing everything.**"

Some people greet each new year with the resolution to read through the Bible by year's end. Most don't make it past March, but for those who do, they oftentimes become so consumed with meeting their reading goal, that the living, breathing word of God is reduced to nothing more than an assignment they cross off each day. Don't let this be you. Better to dwell on a few sacred words of Scripture and incorporate them into your life than to pride yourself for making it through the rousing chapters of Leviticus by the end of February!

One verse at a time, consciously and genuinely incorporated into your daily life, will reap rewards of happiness, the likes of which you've probably never enjoyed before. I know, because I've been blessed by this practice for many years. Most recently, I've adopted Philippians 2:3–4 as my personal challenge verse. It says, "Don't be selfish; don't try to impress others. Be humble, thinking of others as better than yourselves. Don't look out only for your own interests, but take an interest in others, too." (NLT). In just a short time and in some of the most subtle ways, I've already seen God use my efforts to bless others and enrich their lives.

Think of the influence to be had, the good to be done, the blessings to be given in simply claiming a few God-inspired words as your daily guidelines for living. I don't know about you, but the idea of expanding my influence for Christ through just one or two simple verses is exhilarating! My mind races to committing to apply another verse and then another and then ... *wow!* Note to self: remember the *quality* of my witness is infinitely more important than the *quantity* of verses I commit to trying to live out. If this were a tortoise and hare analogy, you'd be most effective taking on the tortoise mind-set, making slow and sometimes almost imperceptible, steady progress toward living the life God wants for you.

You've probably seen the J-O-Y acrostic in which "J" stands for Jesus, "O" stands for others, and "Y" represents you. It's simple enough for a kindergartener to memorize, and yet it sums up the priorities Christ wants us to have and what it takes to have a "Happy to Do It" heart. The amazing thing is that while this is the directive for *us* to have happiness, *we* are the source for our Heavenly Father. You. Me. The grumpy lady down the street. The guy driving like a maniac down the interstate. Hard to believe? Look at Hebrews 12:2: "Let us fix our eyes on Jesus, the author and perfecter of our faith, who for the joy set before him, endured the cross ..." Who was that joy? Unbelievably, it's you and me. And the grumpy lady. And the crazy driver. It's all that and then some. The Savior of the world gave His life on a cross for the sole (or is it soul?!) purpose of paving the way to eternity for us.

Can you imagine that imposing conversation between God and His son, Jesus? The Creator of the universe and His one and only Son having the ultimate heart to heart. It seems "Dad" has some kind of plan and is wanting His Son to work in and sacrifice for the "family business." "Son, My creation needs a Savior. I'd really appreciate it if You'd pay them a visit, live Your life (a short one at that), and then give Your life on a cross for *their* sins," explains God.

And Jesus being … well, Jesus, must have surely replied, "Sure, Dad. Happy to Do It!"

In turn, each day Jesus asks each one of us, "Will you live for Me? Will you be a light and encouragement to the people you meet today, whether they deserve it or not? Will you be someone who makes an impact for My kingdom?"

For me, there is no other acceptable response than, "Happy to Do It."

For bonus content related to this chapter, please visit:
http://www.happytodoit.jlog.com

2

WEIGHT TRAINING

Atkins®.

Nutrisystem®.

South Beach®.

SugarBusters®.

What do all these brand names have in common? They're all "fixes" (most extremely short-lived!) to America's over-the-top and ever-increasing weight problem. I call them fixes because, unless you adopt any of these plans as a long-term lifestyle and integrate them into your everyday life, they are all little more than a temporary fix to a larger (literally!) problem.

As a country, we've long since passed just being *fat*. We're embracing obesity (at least as much as our chubby little arms can!) the way kindergarteners slam down vanilla wafers at snack time! For many of us, morbid obesity is the next stop on this huffin' and puffin' train to Fat City. Not just fat. Not just obese. But *morbidly* obese! So extreme is the obesity crisis in our country that its exponential growth has elevated this destructive condition to the point where it is given *epidemic* status.

Folks, this problem of overconsumption of things that are bad for us goes way beyond just how we look in a bathing suit. This trend of indulging in increasingly harmful habits is doing obvious damage to our outsides, but it is the unseen deterioration of our internal health that is hurting us the most. Not only are we making the outside unsightly (think love handles, muffin tops, and orange peel/cottage cheese thighs), but our continued indulgence in this "live for today: eat, drink, and be happy" lifestyle has become the primary factor in our collective (and greatly accelerated) decline and premature deaths!

Recently, I started feeling a bit convicted about my expanding waistline and my noticeably decreasing stamina on the basketball court, so I decided to get a professional's opinion about the state of my health. I made an appointment at the nationally renowned Cooper Aerobics Clinic in Dallas. So proud was I of my substantial step toward improving my health that I celebrated with a thick, juicy bacon cheeseburger. Hey! I made the appointment … it was a step!

After the day-long battery of tests, measurements, and analyses (with nary a cheeseburger in sight, I might add!), I ended the day with a sit-down consultation with the head doc. Ever the optimist, he led with the good news, "Well, you're in great health …" he paused, waiting for my premature smugness to subside. "You're just overweight *and* out of shape."

Not one significant issue, but two. "Hey doc," I *wanted to say*, "I paid you $2,500 to tell me what I *already* knew? Let's circle back 'round to the part about me being in 'great health.' I'm kind of in need of a little encouragement here—either that or something a little more substantial than the rabbit food they gave me for lunch!"

I held my tongue, shook his hand, and gathered my things (including my plummeting self-worth). During my thirty-minute drive back home, I had time to rehash the doctor's words, warnings, and recommendations and think about what they meant for me. By the time I hit the driveway, I had determined that I had two options at this point: continue on the path I was so comfortably entrenched in at the expense of future health or take a bit of responsibility for my own health and begin integrating a few more wiser choices into the minutes, hours, and days that were fast becoming what I like to refer to as my life.

Mmmmmm … watch my kids graduate or a burger with *extra* bacon … travel with my wife or that *fourth* piece of sausage pizza …toss my grandkids in the air or clean my plate *every* time? The answers were obvious. How it played out, however, was not quite so simplistic.

Since my own personal "day of reckoning" with the undeniable test results and lab analyses laid out before me, I've made some changes in how I view my role in my health. I know, more than ever before, that the quality of my future days is directly related to how I spend my present days. I know that a salad with minimal dressing is lots better for my system than my beloved bacon cheeseburger and fries combo. And I know that walking to and from the refrigerator is not considered serious exercise. I know all these things *in my head.* Science, nutrition, and just plain common sense tell me all these things. But if you're anything like me, sometimes a big bowl of peanut M&Ms and a good action movie win out over elevated triglycerides, HDLs, and the like. I am, as the saying goes, *a work in progress.*

> **To become a sold-out and committed example is mostly a matter of the heart, not my head.**

So what have I ultimately learned from my steps toward healthy living? Though I had long since known it, my experience with taking control of my health through diet, exercise, and well-being drove home to me in a very personal way a very simplistic, but powerful truth: whatever the endeavor before me—be it adopting a healthy lifestyle, being the husband and dad my family needs me to be, or standing strong for Christ during times of blessing and challenge—becoming a sold-out and committed example is mostly a matter of the *heart,* not my *head.*

What It Takes to Shape Up

I wasn't long into this revised lifestyle of making smarter eating choices and pumping some iron when I realized that many of the same principles most of us use to improve our physical health are just as relevant and helpful for getting our spiritual life in optimal shape. If you think about it, both our physical well-being and our spiritual impact are concerned with weight—just different perspectives on what weight really means to each area. Regarding our physical self, weight is, more often than not, viewed negatively. It's not too often that you hear some discouraged and disgruntled woman in a department store dressing room lamenting, "I've just *got* to put on some more weight!" No, friends, for the overwhelming majority of us, we carry too much weight for our frames.

But think about how, outside of our physical shapes, frames, and forms, the word weight is used to connote influence. "He'll make things happen … he'll throw his weight around." Or maybe, "She'll get things done because her vote carries the most weight." Or even, "If they weigh in for us, we'll get the contract because they're so well respected." See the entirely different meaning weight carries in these instances? Unlike someone battling the numbers on the scale, whenever somebody wants to influence others through their words and actions, they are seeking to increase their "weight" in regard to impacting others. And so, I came to realize that, just as I *consciously and intentionally* trained my muscles to lift more weight to improve my physical weight, I also had to *consciously and intentionally* train my "spiritual muscles" to take on more weight and thus, exert more influence on those around me.

Inspired by the parallel between shaping up physically *and* spiritually, I soon found myself spurred on by a newfound intensity and commitment—traits previously foreign to me when faced with a big ol' plate piled high with buffalo wings and the Sunday afternoon football game vs. a fruit salad and a walk to the park and back! As I made a little progress, I became bold enough to take my physical weight training to a new level and hired a personal trainer. And while I'm not saying every time we meet, I jump at the thought of going through the paces with him and his grueling routines, but I have come to appreciate the benefits of doing what he challenges me to do.

In fact, I hadn't been meeting with my trainer too long when I had another "lightning bolt" revelation about the similarity between what his intentions were for my weight and what Jesus' intentions were for my spiritual weight or my influence. Both of them want me to do what they ask of me (whether I want to or not!); both of them know that sometimes it can be a bit painful to stretch beyond your comfort zone, but that once you do so, you're all the stronger for it; both of them know tons more than I do about their respective areas of expertise; and both of them know that to be at my best, my weight (be it physical or spiritual) needs to be in optimal form and continually improving.

And so, just as my change from a burger-lovin' big guy to a slightly evolved conscientious eater has been gradual and is still ever so much a day-to-day process, so also has my lifelong journey from natural-born-sinner to committed Christ-follower. In the short-term, I've got a fit, toned, and energetic trainer to push me to do "one more set" for the sake of my biceps. For the long, long-term (as in eternal!) future, I have the ultimate trainer of all mankind—Jesus, who, no matter what attitude I bring to "work out" each day, still meets and greets me with open arms, a gentle and encouraging spirit, and the promise to provide for me all that I'll ever need.

Not surprisingly, as I've become more committed to my weight-training routines and practices (both physically and spiritually!), I've become more appreciative of the results and rewards the disciplines of both provide. I also have come to realize that, just as my trainer wants me in peak form as a testament to his influence on my life and as a walking endorsement for his influence upon me, Christ also wants me to reflect His unyielding and unwavering influence upon my life and the life-altering changes that await anyone who adheres to His training program.

Though I don't claim to have an exhaustive list, I do find inspiration and encouragement in several specific parallels between physical and spiritual "weight training." Through routines and repetitions of exercises, personal trainers integrate cause-and-effect actions into their workout plans with the intent to stretch and strengthen their clients' muscles. Through the words of Scripture, Christ's admonishments to His followers are also intended to put us through challenging paces with the guarantee of eternal results. Whether your workout is physical, spiritual, or both, to be the best you can be, you can be sure your trainers will challenge you to:

- Identify your weaknesses.
- Improve your flexibility.
- Inventory your diet.
- Increase your cardio.

Identify Your Weaknesses

Though lots of us would like to deny that we have weaknesses, the truth is that we've all got weaknesses. For some of us, our weaknesses are significant and character altering; for others, they're minor by comparison and of manageable consequence throughout our lives. For the more insecure among us, we do just the opposite of denying our weaknesses; we tell every and anyone who will listen what our weaknesses are (come to think of it, isn't that a weakness in itself?) and how ill-suited we are for anything just above breathing. Either extreme—denial or self-wallowing—isn't a healthy option for our physical or spiritual growth.

One of the many tests the docs performed on me during my marathon day of "let's poke, prod, and analyze Randy" at the Cooper Clinic was to measure my hearing. I was especially interested in this test because Elizabeth had been telling me for quite some time that my hearing must be failing me because I didn't seem to respond to her quite as quickly as she thought I should. Not wanting to rock the marital boat, I found it easier to agree with her until I had scientific proof to the contrary.

Needless to say, when the doctor reviewed my hearing test, I listened *extremely* well. "I'm happy to tell you that your hearing is great," the doctor said as he looked over my results. "Reallllly," I said. "Because

my wife is forever telling me that my hearing just isn't what it *should* be. I'll be anxious to tell her the good news."

Picking up on my smug satisfaction, the doctor was quick to comment, "It seems you have something many husbands suffer from … *selective hearing.*"

"Well … yeah," I reluctantly copped to his diagnosis, "but she has *selective submission*, so we're even."

Actually, all of us that claim the title of Christian suffer from both *selective hearing* and *selective submission*. Some of us only show symptoms occasionally, while others of us seem to have a chronic case of selectivity. Our selective hearing shows up when we listen for God's ever-present voice when it's convenient for us. When things are going well and we presumptuously think we've got a handle on the comings and going of our lives, we tend to turn a deaf ear to God's gentle and guiding voice. Let a little chaos and trouble creep into our lives and we're calling up God on speed dial. Like I said, we listen to God only when it's convenient for us.

The same holds true regarding selective submission. If following and obeying what we think to be the commands of the Lord make sense to us and doesn't contradict what we *want* or what we think *should* happen, we're all on board. But let the gentle nudges of the Holy Spirit go against what is popular with the world or what is the easy way out or what allows us to "save face," and all of a sudden, we start to question whether God would really want us to submit in such a seemingly uncomfortable situation. Again, we submit to God when it seems reasonable to *us*, not reasonable to *Him*.

Sometimes we let our weaknesses stand in the way of getting to know God better. We tell ourselves we've blown it as far as being a Christ-like example, so why bother at all? We dwell on our faults and question God's ability to use us in spite of them. We feel limited by our abilities and don't see how they can be of use in Christ's kingdom. We make excuse after excuse about how we're not worthy enough, talented enough, or "religious" enough to be used of and for God. Whatever the excuse or the rationale behind it, the result is the same: we impose limits on God and His incredible, unfathomable, and totally off-the-charts ability to use us for His purpose.

Undoubtedly the apostle Paul had similar doubts, but his deep faith in God's ability to overcome his human shortcomings was evident in Philippians 4:13 when he said, "I can do everything through him who gives me strength." Not just the little things, the easy things, the "quick fixes," but *everything.*

With Christ, everything means *everything.* No exceptions. No small print. No loopholes. E-V-E-R-Y-T-H-I-N-G.

If you apply God's guidance and direction to our shape-up analogy, think of Christ as our own personal trainer. He walks us through challenging exercises, pushes us further than is sometimes comfortable, encourages us when our spirits lag, and talks us through how He wants us to perform. With every exercise He puts us through, He reminds us, "You can do everything I ask of you through My power." There's that word again ... *everything.*

> **With Christ, everything means everything. No exceptions. No small print. No loopholes. E-V-E-R-Y-T-H-I-N-G.**

If, in our most trying of times, we are able to identify our weaknesses and wholly and completely turn them over to God, then we're on the right track toward Christlikeness. It's when we introduce the option of failure, when we only partially commit, when we reduce our efforts to merely *trying* and not *doing*, that we take a step *away* from accomplishing our goals.

Say you were to invite some friends to a party at your place and they respond by saying, "We'll *try* to make it there." You and I both know they don't have the slightest intention of coming to your party. By saying they'll *try*, they're really saying, "We'll think about it and, if we don't get a better offer, we *might* show up ... or if there's not a good movie on at the theater ... or if the cat doesn't need a bath ... or ..." To say they'll *try* is the politically correct thing to say, but it's not exactly a commitment you can bank on.

What if you and I were on a plane, headed for Honolulu, and the captain came on the intercom and announced, "Well, folks, we're approaching our descent, and I gotta tell you, this island runway is some kind of tricky! It's short and narrow and just about runs into the ocean, but don't worry, I'm going to do my level-best to *try* to land this jumbo jet." Try? Did he say "*try*"? I think it's a pretty safe bet that I wouldn't be the only one confessing sins and asking for some double-time forgiveness.

Just like we don't want people to *try* on the really big stuff in life, God doesn't want us to only *try* to be like Him. He wants us to *be* like Him. To try is not good enough for God. To *be* like Christ should always be the goal before us.

Most of us are all too aware of our weaknesses—physically, emotionally, spiritually, and so on. To us, our shortcomings are glaring reminders of our limited abilities, our deficiencies, and our areas in need of some big-time improvement. It's these seeming weaknesses that are just the point of entry that God looks to bless us in. In 2 Corinthians 12:9, Jesus tells Paul, "My grace is enough; it's all you need. My strength comes into its own in your weakness." (The Message)

This was life-changing for Paul, who admitted, "Once I heard that, I was glad to let it (my weaknesses) happen. I quit focusing on the handicap and began appreciating the gift. It was a case of Christ's strength moving in on my weakness. Now I take my limitations in stride, and with good cheer, these limitations that cut me down to size—abuse, accidents, opposition, bad breaks. I just let Christ take over! And so the weaker I get, the stronger I become." (2 Corinthians 12:10, The Message) Now that's a healthy attitude toward embracing your weaknesses!

Improve Your Flexibility

As I get older, I'm more determined than ever to remain reasonably flexible, both physically and spiritually. I've seen way too many people who shut down—both their bodies and their hearts—and they quit being any good to anyone. So I take it in stride when my trainer reminds me to "stretch a little" between my weight-lifting exercises. I've tried telling him that when you buy your clothes in the big and tall department, just moving of any sort is *stretching*, but he doesn't buy it! Still, I try to keep him happy and go through the movements of pushing my muscles just a little bit further each time. It's sometimes tough at the time, but I'm always glad when it's over that I stretched my muscles past their usual resting state. This attention to improving my flexibility makes the tasks of everyday life go smoother and prepares me to do more the next day. The same is true when we make an effort to improve our spiritual flexibility.

Just like I can tell when I haven't stretched my muscles in a while, I can also tell when I haven't stretched myself spiritually. A few days without pushing myself spiritually and getting beyond my small, little world and I find myself quickly becoming close-minded, short-sighted, and judgmental. The Bible is clear about the consequences of passing judgment on others. Romans 2:1 plainly tells us, "You, therefore, have no excuse, you who pass judgment on someone else, for at whatever point you judge the other, you are condemning yourself, because you who pass judgment do the same things."

This reminds me of what my parents used to tell me whenever I would point out (literally!) somebody else's faults. To truly point at something with your "pointer finger," you've got to curl the other three fingers under and when you do so, you end up with three fingers pointing back at you! Wow! Three times the convictions that you're casting forth on others!

Sadly, sometimes it is the people who have been in church the longest who are the most judgmental of those just joining Christ's family. We forget that not everyone knows the books of the Bible forward and back or knows the words to 150 hymns by heart or can quote a relevant Scripture verse for every problem that comes your way. We frequently judge new believers because they're not up to our standards, and we impose unrealistic expectations upon them to get "up to speed," so to speak, in their walk with God. Whenever I hear of or witness longtime Christ-followers engaged in passing judgment on others, I've learned to

intentionally not *judge* their judging but rather *learn* from their actions and re-commit to showing the grace and mercy Christ would have me extend to others.

Because I've been a believer for over forty years, I have hopefully gained some insights into how God works, what He wants of us, and how to grow closer to Him. The spiritual maturity that has come from years and years of growing in Christ has given me a depth of knowledge that new believers don't have the benefit of. By remembering my early days as a Christ-follower and the many, many challenges my faith has seen me through, I am frequently able to draw on my longtime relationship with Christ to help new believers on their own path to developing a deep and meaningful relationship with God.

The years have opened my eyes to the double blessing of helping others in their spiritual growth as I've come to realize that by reaching out and extending a spiritual hand out to people just beginning their walk with Christ, I am also able to improve my spiritual flexibility. The enthusiasm, the questions, and the wonder of people just beginning their Christian walk all challenge me to remain flexible spiritually when I'm with them. Their enthusiasm is contagious and a welcome emotion for someone prone to being comfortable in their beliefs; their questions challenge me to fully understand what and why I believe as I do; and their wonder motivates me to stay fresh in my awe and amazement of all God has done and continues to do for me. In the company of fresh, new believers, I may be the mature one with lots of so-called experience with God, but it is their newfound appreciation for our Heavenly Father and my desire to recapture that for myself that improves my spiritual flexibility like nothing else.

Besides judging others and having unrealistic expectations for new believers, some of us longtime followers have come to the point where we don't even want to associate with nonbelievers. We think it's bad for our image or our reputation to hang out with such *heathens*. Some of us don't just pass on the opportunity to share with them, we all-out avoid contact with non-Christians whenever possible. You could say we boycott them, their actions, and their beliefs. In doing this, we couldn't be further away from where God wants us to be. If Jesus were here amongst us today, He would be the first one out of the church, looking for the lost, and sharing the good news with them. As believers, Jesus expects and commands nothing less from us. He wants us to be people of influence and to use us in the lives of those who have yet to come to know Him.

The New Testament story of Zaccheus, the tax collector, is a great example of Christ's bold and unapologetic walk among sinners. You see, ol' Zaccheus was a shrimp of a guy, a classic case of short-man-syndrome, but he used his position as a tax collector to exert power over those who would have normally dismissed him. So zealous was Zaccheus that he didn't just collect the necessary and appropriate taxes, but he padded most people's "amount due" so as to keep a little off the top for the "make Zac's life easier" fund.

> **As any basic leadership book will tell you, influence based upon position is the lowest level of influence among others because, if you separate the person from the position, all authority goes with it.**

As any basic leadership book will tell you, influence based upon position is the lowest level of influence among others because, if you separate the person from the position, all authority goes with it. The same would have undoubtedly been true for Zaccheus, but he worked his position for all he could until one life-changing encounter with an emboldened messenger: Jesus. As word of Jesus' arrival in Jericho reached the village, the townspeople began lining the road into town to see firsthand the Savior they had heard so much about. Though not a believer at the time, Zaccheus was also curious to see this man called Jesus. Because of the tremendous crowds and his slight stature,

Zaccheus climbed up in a roadside tree to get a glimpse of Jesus as He came through Jericho.

Imagine the little man's shock when Jesus stopped directly in front of the tree, looked upward to him, and said, "Zaccheus, come down immediately. I must stay at your house today" (Luke 19:5). Without hesitation, Zaccheus scrambled down and welcomed Jesus gladly. The townspeople, however, weren't nearly as enthusiastic about Jesus' selection. Knowing the local tax collector as they did, they began to mutter amongst themselves, disparaging Zaccheus' character and claiming, "He has gone to be the guest of a 'sinner'" (Luke 19:7).

Never mind that, as a result of Jesus' choice to visit with a known nonbeliever, there was a complete about-face in Zaccheus' behavior. His life was changed to the point of him donating half of his income to the poor and the repayment of all he overcharged times four! Yes, despite the crowd's judgmental comments and condemnation of Zaccheus' character, Jesus was quick to welcome Zaccheus into the fold of new believers as he told the onlookers, "Today salvation has come to this house, because this man, too, is a son of Abraham. For the Son of Man came to seek and to save what was lost" (Luke 19:9–10).

It's interesting, isn't it, that people today have the same tendencies of those thousands of years ago to cast aspersions and make judgments on those different than them. More interesting is that Jesus' words are just as relevant and applicable to us as they were to the busybodies of Jericho in Zaccheus' day.

Inventory Your Diet

Recently, I was working out with my trainer and he asked me how my diet was going. "Great," I replied. "I like just about everything out there—Burger King®, McDonald's®, Taco Bell®. You name it, and I like it." Suffice it to say, this was *not* the answer he was looking for.

"Listen, Randy," he said as he looked me squarely in the eyes, "you need to take inventory of what you're putting into yourself and start making some healthier choices. It's the only way you're going to significantly impact the results." Yikes! I had been so busy concentrating on the number of reps, maintaining the right workout form, and increasing my heart rate that I had pretty much totally neglected what I was doing to my insides. What's more, I *liked* all those delectable choices from my favorite fast-food restaurants!

When I thought further about the unwelcome words of my trainer, I began realizing that what we put into us goes way beyond just the food we consume. If we're intent on being used by God to influence others on His behalf, we've got to make some seriously healthy choices in regard to what we listen to, what we watch on television and in the movie theaters, and what we search for and explore on the Internet.

The depth of this understanding made me think back to the summer of 1975 when the movie *Jaws* came out in theaters. I was a senior in high school and took Elizabeth, who was my girlfriend at the time. Now I'm a tough guy, but watching that great white shark rip those people apart like rag dolls made an impact that has lasted well beyond the two hours I spent in the theater. It changed the way I looked at the ocean *forever!*

Decades have since passed, but the sound of that ominous music they played as the shark approached in the movie still plays in my head and makes me a little weak in the knees every time I come near a shoreline. (Dut da … dut da … dut da, dut da, dut da … Just two notes into the music, and you know there's trouble coming!) Don't tell me that what we watch on TV, at the movies, and online doesn't impact us. It does in a tremendous way, whether we're conscious of it or not. Healthy choices, whether it be food or media, have to be an intentional option for us if we are to influence others as God would have us to do.

It is also important to take inventory of who we spend much of our time with. It's a proven fact that we reflect many of the lifestyle choices and character traits of those with whom we associate. In short, we *are* our friends. Remember how your parents used to be so concerned about who you hung out with? It's because they knew that as your friends did, you would also. The same holds true, even if you're well beyond junior

high. As adults, we still tend to mirror much of the same attitudes and ideas of our peers; we just wear nicer clothes now.

We are told emphatically to influence others, especially nonbelievers, but our closest associations should be with those who know and love Christ and want the best for us. It is in these friendships that others will stand by you, pick you up when you need a hand, lift you up when you need prayer, and encourage you to be all that God wants you to be. One of the easiest ways to form friendships of this nature is through a church small group or a Bible study. Bonds formed in the security of a small group of believers that meet together on a regular basis for fellowship and Bible study are some of the strongest you'll ever experience. Brothers and sisters in Christ help you to focus on the things of God, not of the world. Philippians 4:8 offers the challenge to fix our minds on what would bring joy to the Lord, not satisfy our selfish natures: "Finally, brothers, whatever is true, whatever is noble, whatever is right, whatever is pure, whatever is lovely, whatever is admirable—if anything is excellent or praiseworthy—think about such things." How blessed to have the direction of God concerning our thoughts and minds so clearly defined!

Increase Your Cardio

It wasn't enough that my trainer challenged me on my dietary choices, but just the other day he wanted to know if I was still upping my cardio workout on a regular basis. "Are you kidding me, man?" I huffed between lifting sets. He wanted to know whether I was running or walking to get my cardio exercise in each day, not *if* I was doing either one! I turned to humor in this no-win interrogation time and told him I was doing all the running I needed to be doing as I ran from the table to the stove for a second helping or from the couch to the fridge during football games. Not surprisingly, he didn't see the humor in my answers!

Just as in the previous examples, increasing our cardio is relevant to both our physical *and* our spiritual health. Staying still, sitting on the sidelines of life, just won't get us to where we need to be. We've got to up our cardio and get "out there" for the Lord.

It's considerably easier to train for the marathon of impacting others for the Lord if we view people as He does: as men and women made in His image, full of sin yet saved by the grace of His slain son. Christ is *passionate* about people, He *cares* about them, and He wants the *best* for them. He also wants us to care as He does.

> " **The problem is that most of us are so self-centered, so selfish, and so into what's going on in our lives that we don't take the time or make the effort to look for ways to help others, to lend a hand, to share our abundance, to be Jesus to them.** "

The problem is that most of us are so self-centered, so selfish, and so into what's going on in our lives that we don't take the time or make the effort to look for ways to help others, to lend a hand, to share our abundance, to *be Jesus* to them. We get caught up in the little ways that others bug us, manipulate us, and even infuriate us at times. We let others make us miserable, and yet, we have the security of knowing Christ loved us first so that we could go forth from that point and love others. First John 4:19 explains Christ's intentions about how and why we are to love: "We, though, are going to love—love and be loved. First we were loved, now we love. He loved us first" (The Message). The ultimate teacher, Jesus Christ, told us what we are to do, showed us what we are to do, and did what we are to do. For me, this certainly takes the guesswork out of what Christ wants of us.

In addition to this simple plan for how to handle our dealings with others, however challenging they may be, we are also to continue along this path of passion for others until we reach Heaven. It's not something that can be done and checked off of our respective to-do lists and move on to something else. It is an ongoing, perpetual challenge that we are to meet every day of our lives. Think of it as the ultimate IOU between us and God: we work on repayment all our days on earth in exchange for the unfathomable gift of eternity in Heaven with Him. This was best explained in Romans 13:8–10 as Paul tells us, "Don't run up debts, except for the huge debt of love you owe each other. When you love others, you complete what the law has been after all along … Love other people as well as you do yourself. You can't go wrong when you love others. When you add up everything in the law code, the sum total is love" (The Message).

God's purpose for you and me is to build up a life of influence through loving others. He wants it to be a life that honors Him and pleases Him in every area of our life—by identifying our weaknesses, improving our flexibility, taking inventory of what we take in, and increasing our passion for people. If we commit to doing this, God promises to change the world *through* us and *around* us. All He asks is that we stand ready and willing to be used *by* Him and *for* Him. It's a training program that offers a lifetime membership with our own intensely *personal* trainer.

For bonus content related to this chapter, please visit:
http://www.happytodoit.jlog.com

Happy to Do It

3

LIGHTS, CAMERA, ACTION

You just never know when people are watching you. In fact, Elizabeth tells me one of the laws of the universe is that when you're looking your worst—grubbed-out sweats (you know the ones with the bleach stain on them!), worn out sneakers, no make-up (at least for her!), and a bad hair day—is when you're certain to run into at least three people you know at the grocery store! You may be just running in for a gallon of milk for the kids' breakfast, but you can be sure you'll see people you know! And they'll want to stop and talk ... and talk. Been there. Done that.

I had a front-row seat to a lesson on the importance of our lifestyle as a witness on a recent business trip. While waiting in the gate area to catch a connecting flight back home, I watched as one man blasted the gate agent for the delay in boarding and consequently the take-off for departure. Seems he had a meeting to get to and he was none too pleased. I didn't really grasp much of the conversation, but as it reached a crescendo, everyone, and I mean *everyone*, in the gate area could hear his parting shot, "Well, if you don't know, then who can I talk to?"

When we were eventually called to board the plane, Elizabeth and I headed to our seats and *blessings of all blessings,* guess who was seated directly across the aisle from me? You guessed it! Mr. "The-

World-Revolves-Around-Me." I could have sworn there was still steam coming from his ears when I took my seat. Knowing this guy's brief history, I decided to pull the universal "don't-talk-to-me-I'm-a-serious-businessman" tactic and avoid all avenues of communication. No courtesy nod. No "glad we're *finally* leaving" commiserating comment. And certainly no eye contact. Yessiree, I was the picture of "leave-me-alone" stoicism at its best. Not that I'm necessarily proud of it, but my "don't bug me" look can stop one of those persistent mall kiosk salespeople in their tracks! What can I say? We all have our special talents!

So I'm in social lock-down mode as I settle into my seat, pull out my laptop, and open my Bible to begin preparing for the sermon I'm supposed to preach on Sunday. Don't worry—in retrospect, I have been sufficiently convicted by the Holy Spirit to see the irony of my actions and reactions—a would-be preacher preparing a message on reaching people and being the light of the world while *intentionally* ignoring someone seated eighteen inches from me! I'm not five minutes into reviewing my notes and looking for a Scripture reference when Mr. Happy-Pants sees my Bible.

"That's an interesting book," he says.

"Yes … yes, it is an interesting book," I echo.

"So, uh, what are your plans with it?" he asks.

"Well, my pastor at Fellowship Church has asked me to preach for him this Sunday, and I'm just trying to get my thoughts together about what I might talk about," I tell him with little elaboration.

"Ed Young at Fellowship Church?" he pushes. "I know Ed. That's a great church. Say, I'm in ministry, too!"

It was all I could do to contain my surprise, but I managed an even-toned reply and, for the next thirty-five minutes, he passionately told me how much he loved God, loved working with pastors, and loved working with church staffs. When we finished visiting, I had to laugh when I saw the book he had brought along to read: *Loving Time.* I'm thinking that gate agent he so colorfully spoke to had anything but a *loving time,* but that's another issue.

From the gate area to her adjacent seat throughout our journey, Elizabeth had watched the whole scene play out with my new acquaintance. To her credit, she didn't say a single word while he was in earshot, but three steps off the jet way, she couldn't contain herself any longer. "I can't believe that guy!" she exclaimed. "There he was, in front of fifty to seventy-five people waiting at the gate—waiting for the *same* flight he was waiting for, with things to do and places to be, just like *him*—and he was more interested in what was good for *him* rather than letting the light of God shine in his life." My bride is nothing if not direct.

She was tough on him, but she was 100 percent right. This man had an audience of several dozen people, all wanting the same thing he wanted, and he chose to disparage and insult the company representative in a loud and offensive manner. This guy was shining his light all right, just not the kind of light I suspect Jesus wants shined on His behalf. Scripture tells us that Jesus presented Himself as "the light of the world" in John 8:12 and promised "whoever follows me will not walk in darkness, but will have the light of life." He then transfers the responsibility to be the light to each of us as His followers in Matthew 5:14 as He tells His disciples, "*You* are the light of the world ..." From God's lips to our hearts, the responsibility to *live for* and *live as* Christ is ours—whether our flight is on time or not.

> **You are the light of the world.**

In the verses that follow, we are commanded to use our light as a means of drawing people near to us in order that they may come to see the Father in us: "Neither do people light a lamp and put it under a bowl. Instead they put it on its stand, and it gives light to everyone in the house. In the same way, let your light shine before men, that they may see your good deeds and praise your Father in Heaven" (vv. 15–16). I grew up going to Vacation Bible School and church camp, and one of

the old standbys when it came to songs was "This Little Light of Mine."
This is how the words went:

> This little light of mine, I'm gonna let it shine,
> This little light of mine, I'm gonna let it shine,
> This little light of mine, I'm gonna let it shine,
> Let it shine, let it shine, let it shine …
> Hide it under a bushel, NO! I'm gonna let it shine,
> Hide it under a bushel, NO! I'm gonna let it shine,
> Hide it under a bushel, NO! I'm gonna let it shine,
> Let it shine, let it shine, let it shine …
> Don't let Satan blow it out, NO! I'm gonna let it shine,
> Don't let Satan blow it out, NO! I'm gonna let it shine,
> Don't let Satan blow it out, NO! I'm gonna let it shine,
> Let it shine, let it shine, let it shine.

If you've heard the song, you know it's got a catchy rhythm with an easy refrain, but its message is so very compelling. As Christ-followers, we've got the Light leading us and within us; it is ours to share and ours to guard, and whether we realize it or not, those without such a blessing are watching to see whether we burn strong and brightly or spit, sputter, and flicker when the smallest of winds cross our paths.

I found myself in the middle of some of Satan's gale force winds trying their darndest to douse my light on yet another flight just weeks after my encounter with "Mr. Grump-Turned-Great-Sermon-Illustration." Elizabeth and I had just gotten to curbside check-in, when I suddenly realized I had left my cell phone at home. Now, I'm not what you'd call an *addict,* but let's just say I seldom go anywhere without my cell phone. And I certainly wouldn't go out of town for four days without my mobile link to all things important to me!

We had fifty-five minutes until flight time and, since we're only eight minutes from the airport, it was a no-brainer: we would return home, get the phone, and arrive back at the gate in plenty of time to catch our flight. The eight-minute trip turned into a fifteen-minute trip due to our misfortune of being trapped behind the absolute *slowest* car on the highway. The once-empty security checkpoint was now backed up, with a line zig-zagging around four dividers. We made it through, caught one of the souped-up golf carts (normally reserved for handicapped or elderly travelers), spilled our carry-on off the back, and ended up grabbing everything we could and running to the gate, only to be greeted by an all-too-cheery-for-the-moment gate agent blocking the jet way entrance.

"I'm so sorry, Mr. Draper," she greeted us, "but it's within ten minutes of flight time, and we can no longer allow any passengers to board the aircraft. If you'll check your ticket, you'll see that's been our policy for over twenty years."

"Twenty years?" I was sooooo trying not to beg, plead, or whine. "How come you're choosing to enforce it *now?*"

"Ever since 9/11, it's been in effect," she explained.

Game. Set. Match.

I knew I had no valid argument to counter national security provisions. And then in a moment that can only be described as spiritual lucidity, I remembered what I'm challenged to be: the light! I'm sure the gate agent thought I had gone schitzo on her, but in a moment of conviction right before her eyes I became a gracious, understanding, and ridiculously accommodating passenger.

We caught the next flight several hours later and, just as I was indulging in a bit of self-congratulatory "way-to-be-the-light" back slappin', the air conditioning went off on the plane *before we ever took off!* It was 110 degrees in Dallas in July, probably ten to fifteen degrees hotter out on the tarmac, and the blasted A/C breaks! It was some kinda hot in that sealed-off, stifling tube sitting still on the stretch of concrete that had suddenly come to resemble a mirage. You know the kind of hot where you sweat and you're not even moving? It was that kind of hot … and then some. Just breathing, I could feel the sweat beads form on my forehead before they all joined together to rush down my face. I could tell every sweat gland in my body was working overtime and I was fading fast! Instead of giving in to my tendency to rush the door for some fresh air, I put my creative energies to work and penned this re-write of "This Little Light of Mine":

> This little light of mine, I'm gonna let it shine,
> Hide it when I leave my cell phone home, NO! I'm gonna let it shine.
> Hide it when the traffic is really slow, NO! I'm gonna let it shine,
> Hide it when the security lines are long, NO! I'm gonna let it shine.
> Hide it when I miss my plane (because of the ten-
> minute rule!), NO! I'm gonna let it shine,
> Hide it when I'm sweatin' like a dog, NO! I'm gonna let it shine.
> Hide it when I'm on the trip from ... well, NO! I'm gonna let it shine,
> Let it shine, let it shine, let it shine!

Okay, so my sarcasm got the better of me when I re-wrote the lyrics. Just know that, at the time, this was a healthy and creative outlet for me to air my frustrations. I had learned the importance of shining for others from Mr. Grumpy on the previous flight. Since then, I've studied up on this challenge to be the light and have found that the Bible has quite a lot to say about *how* we are to live this out. I've identified five of what I consider to be the most important qualities we are to possess if we're serious about letting our light "so shine."

Let your light shine.

We Are to Have Love That Is Unconditional

Ever notice how some people are just easier to love than others? Maybe it's because they do something for us, give something to us, or benefit us in some manner. At the very least, they're enjoyable to be around and seem to appreciate our finer qualities. We don't have to think twice about extending our love to them. But the Bible tells us that it's the *other* people we're also supposed to share our love with, too. You know the kinds I'm talking about—the ones who don't just see eye-to-eye with you, but make a point out of causing you angst, anger, and frustration. The type of people who, if you had your way, you might never even see again, much less engage in any type of conversation with. It's these very folks that God wants us to extend our precious love toward.

Look at Matthew 5:43–44 and you'll see the clarity of Christ's words regarding this: "You have heard that it was said, 'Love your neighbor and hate your enemy.' But I tell you: Love your enemies and pray for those who persecute you…" This counterintuitive kind of love is *agape* love, and it's the kind of love that is probably the hardest kind to practice because it is offered unconditionally, with no strings attached. Not surprisingly, it is the *exact* kind of love our Heavenly Father rains down on us 24/7. It's not easy, but it *is* what's required of us for authentic Christlikeness.

We Are to Have Integrity That Is Irreplaceable

Before we come to know the Lord, integrity is an admirable quality to adopt. However, *after* we lay claim to Christ's family, integrity is a nonnegotiable. It's a "have-to," not a "want-to." It's a requirement, not a request. It's one of those traits that is completely and undeniably inseparable from those of us who wear the honorable title of Christ-follower. It's probably the single most identifying character trait that nonbelievers look for in believers. Whether in family relationships, friendships, or business dealings, unquestionable, irreplaceable integrity is a hallmark of Christ-followers the world over.

Integrity is the fruit that comes from being filled with Christ's light. We can't help but display honorable behavior when we really grasp what Christ has done *for* us and given *to* us. Observe the "before-and-after" example Ephesians 5:8–9 speaks of: "For you were once darkness, but now you are light in the Lord. Live as children of light for the fruit of the light consists in all goodness, righteousness, and truth …" See there? When you get the one (the light), you get the other (integrity).

I saw just how powerful personal integrity can be when I dealt with many of my creditors during the downfall of my homebuilding business. One supplier in particular seemed to take stock of my seemingly surprising practices. I owed one of our local concrete companies thousands and thousands of dollars when my company finally went under. And since Elizabeth and I opted not to file bankruptcy, the debts remained for many, many years. Once I began building another business and began receiving a regular income, I resumed paying them—little by little. Month after month, I paid them what I could, slowly chipping away at my massive IOU.

Years went by and my payments continued. One day, I looked up from my desk to see the sales rep from the company standing in front of me. After we exchanged pleasantries, he seemed to change his countenance and said, "You know, Randy, we really appreciate you continuing to pay on your bills, but enough time has passed such that you don't *have* to pay them anymore."

I must have looked like what he said didn't compute because he was quick to explain. "I know. I know. You want to keep paying it back because of what's in here," he said as he pointed to his heart. All I could do was nod in agreement.

That moment was only topped by the day I made the final payment on my longest-standing bill. Of the three company owners, one was a believer, and he called me later on the day I made the last payment. "Randy," he said, "I want to thank you for seeing this debt through 'til the end. You'll never understand what this did for me. You see, my other two partners don't know Christ and they told me, 'That preacher's boy will never pay us back.' But you, Randy, have been such a witness to my partners by paying this back in full and for doing the right thing by our company." Let me tell you, at that moment, every sacrifice my family had made for years and *years* was worth it to know that others had seen the light through my actions. It wasn't easy. In fact, it was tougher than I ever dreamed it would be, but I wouldn't have settled for any other resolution.

We Are to Have Grace That Is Unimaginable

It's not enough just to love those who are difficult to love, but we are commanded to forgive even those who it is next to impossible to forgive. By showing this grace to those who have hurt us, we are honoring Christ as few people, believers included, can comprehend. It seems contrary to our gut-level, wanna-get-even reaction to extend our forgiveness to our trespassers, yet that is exactly what Christ commands us to do in Matthew 6: 14–15: "For if you forgive men when they sin against you, your Heavenly Father will also forgive you. But if you do not forgive men their sins, your Father will not forgive your sins." I'm not saying I *want* to forgive the guy at work who "stole" the big account from me or the distant relative who dinged my back bumper last Thanksgiving, but if that's what it takes to receive Jesus' forgiveness for my zillion-and-a-half sins, then count me in. Think about it this way: the tradeoff of a few minutes of honorable humility with your offender in return for eternity with the King. When I look at it that way, the very *least* I can muster is some occasionally "unimaginable grace" for the sake of my Savior.

We Are to Have Humility That Is Motivational

I heard about this preacher who had written a book and was so enthralled with its publication that he took every opportunity to talk about what he considered to be a literary masterpiece. Sunday morning sermons, Lions' Club invocations, and even formal ceremonies were fair game for the pastor to artfully weave some reference to his book into his speech. Despite this sometimes annoying habit, he was still considered a very effective speaker and was regularly booked for speaking engagements. When it came time for his denominational convention, the organizers were faced with a dilemma. As a recognized author, they wanted him to address the crowd but were determined to keep him "on topic" and not have him digress to the points within his book.

"I know," said one of the committee organizers, "let's get him to pray instead of formally addressing the crowd! That way, he'll have to talk to God and won't be able to talk about his book!"

Everyone was in complete agreement, and the pastor was booked. The group gave little more thought to the issue until the pastor took the podium, adjusted the microphone, and seemed to settle in for a lengthy stay. "Dear God," he began, "Thou who has also written a book like myself, You know as I do that the people we most enjoy are those who possess a humble spirit. Those who consume their days and their thoughts with concerns only of themselves aren't honoring to you because they only speak of those they love the most. And Lord, we know those people to be me, myself, and I. Amen." This guy is living proof of the old saying, "Where there's a will, there's a way!"

Sadly, this kind of false humility is anything but motivational when it comes to being Christlike. In fact, Christ was the original and the ultimate in other-centered living … and dying. He set the example and commanded those who came after Him to follow His lead. The apostle Paul issues the challenge in Philippians 2:3–5, "Do nothing out of selfish ambition or vain conceit, but in humility consider others better than yourselves. Each of you should look not only to your own interests, but also to the interests of others. Your attitude should be the same as that of Christ Jesus …" It may not seem like it at the time, but humility of spirit almost always gives others in its presence a moment of personal reflection. Not everyone will 'fess up to thinking it's the honorable response, but many will, and in the quiet moments afterward, they will consider a humble response to be the most admirable reaction possible. If they see and learn from it, great; if not, you've done what's commanded unto you, and ultimately, we're all just playing for an audience of one.

We Are to Have Thankfulness That Is Inspirational

Even in the roughest of times, we are to be thankful for all that God has placed in or allowed into our lives. A glance at Paul's later years spent in a Roman prison, chained and constrained, would be enough for most of us to ditch the "silver lining" theory. But faithful to the end, Paul sang praises of thanksgiving despite his horrific circumstances. It seems no mental or physical abuse could render him thankless. When I compare my circumstances to Paul's, well … there's really no comparison. And when I'm honest enough to admit that and take to heart his sold-out contentment and thankfulness, I see an example I can only hope to aspire to, and that, friends, is truly inspirational.

When we intentionally seek to have all of these qualities—Love, Integrity, Grace, Humility, and Thankfulness—LIGHT—our light will shine like a beacon to the lost and looking. That's how it was with Jesus and how He wants it to be with us. People who have yet to experience the indescribable peace of Christ's saving grace are living their lives in a spiritual darkness, and many don't even realize it. They don't have a clue about how dark their daily existence is until they're exposed to the light, and that's where we come in.

> **We rarely find ourselves in the depth of complete and utter darkness.**

Think about the darkest place you know, maybe a closet, a basement, or under the bed. Even in the darkest spot in your house, there's usually at least a little bit of light shining either from just beneath the door, between the drapery panels, or through the slats of the shutters. We rarely find ourselves in the depth of complete and utter darkness. It's been more than forty years since I first experienced what it meant to be in total and profound darkness, yet the moment has stayed with me for a lifetime.

We were on a family vacation at Carlsbad Caverns, New Mexico. We had made our way to the deepest cave on the trail and were surrounded by the amazing formations that seemed to seep from the ceiling and spring from the ground. It was cool, dank, and just a little bit eerie. I loved it! After we had our share of stalactites and stalagmites and our guide had explained the history of the cave, he said, "I'm going to flip the switch to turn off these overhead fluorescent lights that light our path. When I do, you'll experience darkness like you've probably never seen before because, at this deep, deep level, there is absolutely no outside light that can penetrate this far down. I would encourage you to put your hand in front of your face in the darkness to get a true feel for just how dark this kind of absolute darkness can be."

As he spoke, the kids in our group wiggled with excitement and the adults became a bit uneasy for the moment and then … flip! All was black. Really, really, *really* black. My brother, sister, and I giggled and tried to "goose" one another in the darkness and just like the guide had said, we held our hands up to our faces and saw *nothing!* It was the most remarkable experience because you *knew* your hand was there; you could hear it if you snapped, feel the air move if you waved it back and forth, and maybe even smell it if you were an eight-year-old boy like me—but no matter how hard you strained your eyes, you absolutely could not see your hand. As a kid, I remember thinking how awesome it was in the cool, quiet, darkness and wishing my bedroom at home would ever get this dark. "Man, this is *cool!*" I said to my brother, "This is as good as it gets!"

It was just a brief moment of millions on the continuum of my childhood, and yet, the significance of that impenetrable darkness made an impact that has lasted a lifetime. That darkness was novel and relaxing, but that was only because I knew it was temporary. I knew the lights would soon come back on and flood the area with enough light to lead us to the opening. I also knew that once back in the light, I would be able to see and all would be well again. Had I separated from the group, been left down below while the rest of my family returned to ground level, and was alone to fend for myself in the pitch black, I would have been afraid, lonely, and wanting someone, *anyone,* to shed some light my way. That's exactly how it is with dozens of people we come into contact with daily. They are afraid, lonely, and desperate for someone, *anyone,* to bring light to their dark and confusing world. It is with such as these that our blessed light shines the brightest and brings the most glory to God.

Different Kinds of Light

The brightness and intensity of our personal lights are usually a reflection of the depth and maturity of our walk with the Lord. If we are to be our most effective in shining God's light for others to find their way, it stands to reason that our focus should be on projecting the strongest, most laser-intensive focused light we can find within us.

When I consider all the different kinds of light available to us today, it's astounding. However strong or weak, direct or diffused, hot or cool—you name it, and there's a light to your liking. Among the weakest of lights is the glow from a single candle. Think of a three-inch birthday candle and the slightest bit of light that comes from it. One breath and it's extinguished. Christ-followers who come to church only on the traditional religious holidays like Christmas and Easter make me think of people whose light is about as strong as a birthday candle. It shines and flickers for a moment, but its impact doesn't last any longer than it takes to sing "Happy Birthday."

Christ-followers with lots of head knowledge of Jesus but little heart understanding of Him remind me of flashlights because when you're holding a flashlight, all the light comes from the "head" of it and they're pulled out in a case of emergency. There's one big end, the head end, and that's where the light shoots out of—not the guts, the inner workings, the "heart" of the light—just the head. I've also known some Christ-followers who best resemble a strobe light in their walk with the Lord. They're off, then on, then off again. They may be white hot for Jesus one day and not shining at all the next. Their brightness is irregular, impossible to predict, and eventually causes a headache to all who are around it too long.

Of all the lights we've got available to us, I think it is the floodlight that most closely resembles what God would have us be to the world. He wants the strength and intensity of a floodlight and its ability to pierce through darkness for miles ahead. If you're anywhere near a floodlight, you just can't help but be literally drenched in light. Stand in the path of a floodlight and you'll be covered—head to toe, front to back, up one side and down the other—in light that pours from its source.

Ask yourself which kind of light you most resemble right now. What about when things aren't always so great? What about when they are? And most importantly, what kind of light do you *want* to resemble? I play a kind of mental game with myself that helps me stay focused on being an authentic floodlight whenever I meet and greet people. Because so many of us (myself included!) greet each other with the universal, "What's up?" intro, I have conditioned myself to hear it more as, "Watts up?" Just by thinking of a light's wattage and its potential for brightness, whenever I'm asked, "What's up," I think, "Watt's up?" and I'm immediately reminded of my challenge to shine like Jesus wherever I find myself. It's goofy, I know, but I'll take anything I can get if it'll help me be more like Jesus!

> **If we're plugged in, we shine at our brightest and without any interruption of service.**

The final thing we've all got to remember as we set out to shine and light the darkness is, as instruments of illumination, we are only as strong as our connection to our power source. If we're plugged in, we shine at our brightest and without any interruption of service. If we're charged up and then become unplugged for a bit, we'll shine for a season but will soon dim and eventually go out without renewal from our source. Ask yourself, what use is a floodlight if it's not plugged in? It might make a good doorstop, but can you really think of any other good use for it if it's not giving off light?

I experienced being separated from my power source the last time I vacuumed. I had my iPod cranked up and my ear buds stuffed in snuggly when I set out to vacuum the den. I was putting everything I had into it, moving chairs, ottomans, and coffee tables, while I was rocking out to "Earth, Wind, and Fire" (Greatest Hits, Vol. II—don'tcha know!). I was just about to finish when Elizabeth came from behind and tapped me on the shoulder.

"What are you doing?" she asked.

"What do you mean, 'What am I doing?'"

"Well, apparently, you're just dragging the vacuum across the floor and not picking anything up, because you're not plugged in!"

I must confess that my first thought at this point was, *Will I get half-credit on the husband score sheet for effort?* I was so wrapped up in what was just relevant to me (namely singing along to one of the greatest bands ever!) that I didn't even realize I wasn't doing what I set out to accomplish. I was going through the motions, and it certainly *looked* like I was doing what I intended to do, but a closer look revealed absolutely no good coming from my intense but unplugged efforts. That's just how it is for our witness when we pull free from the perfect power source and try to do things on our own. Our efforts are futile, tiresome, and yield dismal results.

Don't waste your energies, talents, and time trying to do what is impossible apart from God. Plug into His supernatural charge and your light will shine better and farther than it's ever shone before. It's okay if you're not to the floodlight stage yet. You'll get there by charging your light a little bit at a time and remembering that a floodlight is nothing more than just a lot of little lights shining in one direction.

For bonus content related to this chapter, please visit:
http://www.happytodoit.jlog.com

.

4

RADAR LOVE

Remember the quiet and peaceful setting of *Mister Rogers Neighborhood*? Everyone got along with *everyone*, the trees were always in bloom, and Mister Rogers *never* stepped in a "land mine" of dog poop! Of course it was perfect—it was on TV! Every once in a while I'll wish for such a perfect little world, but then one of my boys will give me a big bear hug and *burp*, "I love you, man!" and I realize we aren't anywhere close to Mayberry.

A few years ago, Elizabeth and I had a real-life encounter that revealed to us that, even in the most seemingly perfect neighborhoods, life is full of people needing the redeeming love of Jesus Christ. For us, our experience was literally a matter of life and death for a young woman who was walking that fine line between living and abandoning all hope.

We were at the University Park home of my in-laws celebrating a milestone anniversary. If you live within the Dallas/Ft. Worth metroplex, you know the University Park/Highland Park neighborhoods are the most prestigious real estate in this part of the state. People move into these neighborhoods simply for the zip code and the social presence it conveys. Lawns are carefully maintained by crews of gardeners. Housekeepers come daily into "the bubble" and dutifully catch the public transportation back home at the end of each day. The social registry is the only phone book necessary for many. And yet on this particular night, all of these outward trappings of success and accomplishment fell by the wayside.

We had just sat down to dinner when the doorbell rang. Because she was seated closest to the door, Elizabeth jumped up and answered the door while our hostess began serving the plates. To really picture this in your mind, you need to realize that the dining room was adjacent to the front entryway, but the way the door opened, it completely blocked any of us from seeing who or what was standing on the front porch.

Suddenly serious, Elizabeth leaned into the dining room and frantically stated, "You all are not going to believe this, but there's a girl on the front porch who shot herself and she's bleeding to death!"

It would help to know at this point that my wife is the number one prankster of all time. She can plot, plan, and pull off whatever the situation calls for if it means pulling one over on someone—especially me. Years of being victimized by her "gotchas" had made me more than just a little bit leery of believing her whenever the story was even remotely outlandish.

'C'mon, Elizabeth," I pleaded. "We just sat down to eat this beautiful meal that your mom has worked on all day long. Enough, already!"

"I'm serious! Call 911 *now!*" she snapped back.

Almost a decade of marriage had taught me one thing: when the tone of my wife's voice gets serious, she isn't fooling around. She meant business! So we all jumped into action and began helping out however we could. Somebody called 911. I grabbed some towels to help slow the bleeding. Somebody else held her head, and someone went to the curb to wave the ambulance in.

The emergency crew was there within minutes and immediately began administering care to save the girl/woman. In all the chaos and through her completely disheveled appearance, it was hard to determine how old she was. Eighteen? Twenty-five? Thirty-two? We didn't know her name, where she came from, or what had motivated her to attempt to take her own life. We did know she was in a world of hurt—physically, emotionally, and spiritually. I'll never forget the look on her scared and tear-stained face as she grabbed Elizabeth's hand and pleaded, "Help me. I don't want to die. I want to live. I've made a mistake."

> **" Every encounter we have with others has the potential to be life-saving. "**

Elizabeth and I know it was no accident that this girl came to her parent's home the exact evening we were there. This girl, just like every other person we come in contact with, was divinely placed in our lives to minister to however she needed it most. In this instance, it was truly a matter of giving life-saving support. If you really, really think about it, it's like that with everyone we meet: every encounter we have with others has the potential to be life-saving. Most of the time these experiences won't involve blood and guts, but that doesn't make them any less life-saving. Most people have their physical existence under control. It's the life-saving, spend-eternity-in-Heaven meetings with others that most of us have the chance to be a part of every single day. All we have to do is be on the lookout and practice what I call *radar love*.

Radar Love Is the Right Kind of Love

You know how it is when a storm is moving into your area and the weatherman interrupts the show you're watching to tell you where the approaching storm is and when it will hit? When I was a kid, the radar screen was nothing more than a few concentric circles with a line of light sweeping over blurry towns and cities. Now the radar at our local station is so precise it can pinpoint *to the minute* when a storm is going to reach a specific intersection. The satellites are so laser-focused that they can see who's got a pool in their backyard and who needs to water their rosebushes.

I think God's love is a lot like *radar love* because He has all of us on His screen; He knows at any given moment what is going on in our lives; He's there tracking us and loving us every step of the way. Whatever we do, we can't run off of God's radar. And as long as we're on His radar, He's showing us His radar love. Like the pinpoint accuracy of the satellites tracking the storms, God's love is laser-focused upon each and every one of us—believers and nonbelievers, big sinners and little sinners— anyone with a breath left within him or her.

When we make a decision to follow Christ and adopt His ways and motives for our lives, radar love becomes the law for us. As the ultimate authority in our lives, Christ's ways become *our* ways. And to make sure we've got all the necessary "equipment," we're given our own unique radar screen to track and be on the alert for those God puts on our screen. It's His way of making His followers part of His plan to reach people. Because God is *God,* He didn't have to involve us in accomplishing His plan; He *wanted* to make us a part of fulfilling His mission on earth. It's something we "get" to do, not "have" to do.

Throughout our days, God places people on our radar screens for the sole purpose of having us demonstrate the love of Christ into their lives. They may be facing a particularly tough time with circumstances much like something we've experienced before. Who better to understand than one who has gone before them? They may not know of any other believers at their work, in their neighborhood, or among their friends. Who better to demonstrate the difference that Christ has made in their life than someone who has tried it both ways? They may be curious about "gettin' religion," but they're freaked out by all the thees and thous in the Bible. Again, who is best suited to show them a different translation of God's word that makes the stories of the Bible suddenly seem relevant? It's you, my friend. It's me. It's anyone who has trusted Christ and who is now entrusted by Christ to show *radar love* to every blip on their screen.

Luke 10 tells of a young lawyer intent on questioning Jesus about the specifics of getting into Heaven. "Teacher," he asked, "what must I do to inherit eternal life?" (v. 25).

Jesus knew the man knew the answer and so asked for his interpretation of Christ's words. The lawyer replied in verse 27, "Love the Lord your God with all your heart and with all your soul and with all your strength and with all your mind; and, Love your neighbor as yourself." As expected, the young man answered precisely correct, yet still was not satisfied, so he pushed for more specifics. "And who is my neighbor?" he pressed (v. 29).

He was asking what all of us want to know—"Who's going to love me as much as they love themselves? Who's going to show *me* that kind of selfless love? Who would ever put *me* before themselves?" You've had that thought, too. I certainly have. We don't like admitting that we're sometimes so me-focused, but we've all "been there, done that" on plenty of occasions.

As He was frequently inclined to do, Jesus used a story to explain what it means to "love your neighbor as yourself." He told the story of the Good Samaritan to illustrate His point. In doing so, Jesus recounted the tale of the man traveling from Jerusalem to Jericho who fell into the hands of robbers. After they had stripped and beaten him, they left him in the roadside ditch for dead. While lying there, the injured man was first passed by a priest and then a Levite, both of whom crossed over to the other side of the road to ignore his needs. It wasn't until a Samaritan man passed by and took pity on the badly beaten up man that he received any care. The Samaritan tended to the man's injuries, took him to the nearest inn, and paid for his lodging, all before continuing on his original journey.

It's worth noting that Jesus never directly answered the lawyer's question regarding who *his* neighbor was but instead challenged the man to understand *whose* neighbor he was to be. To be certain his point was received, when Jesus finished the story, he asked the lawyer which of the three passersby was a neighbor to the man. "The one who had mercy on him," replied the lawyer. Pleased that His student had grasped the point of His lesson, Jesus told the man in verse 37, "Go and do likewise."

On the surface, the story is significant enough to make its point, but the greater meaning was not lost on the young lawyer. He knew the cultural mores of the time and he knew that Jews and Samaritans did everything in their power to avoid any contact with the other. These were two very distinct societies that hated one another with a vengeance, so for the Samaritan in the story to go out of his way to lend aid to a Jew was just short of unbelievable. The significance of the Samaritan's willingness to cross cultural boundaries to help a man in need, regardless of his ethnicity, was a huge move and meant to impress upon the lawyer (as well as us) that a neighbor is anyone in our sphere of influence in need. Jesus intended this story to show *radar love* knows no boundaries. It also knows no valid excuses. *Radar love* is not optional for believers. It is the law of our lives.

Radar love is also like the passport of Heaven. Think about when you use a passport and what it records. You need it when you travel to foreign lands, and when you've used it, you have the identifying marks of each place you visited. *Radar love* is a lot like that. It shows we're a citizen of Christ's kingdom, that we've visited Christ's promised land of forgiveness, redemption, and salvation, and our lives have become the identifying mark that we've been touched by Christ. Sure the bumper stickers, the cross necklaces, and the Christian t-shirts make the claim that we're believers, but it is in our everyday acts that our lives speak what is real.

> **Radar love is also like the passport of Heaven.**

In 1 John 4:20–21, John tells us that our love for God has to go well beyond claims to follow a yet-unseen Savior: "If anyone says, 'I love God,' yet hates his brother, he is a liar. For anyone who does not love his brother, whom he has seen, cannot love God, whom he has not seen. And he has given us this command: Whoever loves God must also love his brother." This is the essence of *radar love,* a love that is willing to get dirty, to sacrifice self, and to put others first as God sees fit to place them on our radar screen.

Though I might get some English teachers arguing with me, I maintain that *radar love* is a verb. I know, I know ... I learned all about the different parts of speech in junior high just like everyone else, but *radar love* is *not* a person, place, or thing. It is action ... or nothing at all. It's not about talking and preaching; it's about acting and practicing. For *radar love* to have its maximum impact, we must demonstrate it to others, not just talk about it. First John 3:18–19 explains that words are simply not enough to fully represent Christ in our lives: "Dear children, let us not love with words or tongue but with actions and in truth. This then is how we know that we belong to the truth ..."

If you're fully engaged in practicing *radar love,* it should be evident in all that you do and all that you are. Is it readily seen in your actions? Does your conversation speak of it? Does your countenance reflect Christ within you? If you've committed your remaining days to following Christ, your whole life should stand as a testament to Jesus' empowering love because it is a love to be shared, not kept within.

It's not always convenient to practice *radar love.* Our opportunities for showing it sometimes come at what we consider to be the most inconvenient time possible, and yet, that's what it's all about—putting our agenda second to the needs of others. I have to regularly remind myself that those who seek me out for assistance or those whom I come in contact with who present a need didn't cross my screen by accident. They are present in my life because God has allowed them to be.

It's also not always easy to practice *radar love.* Some of the people God puts on my radar screen are just downright contentious. Some of them are the type of people I wouldn't normally cross the room to talk to were it not for the conviction of the Lord. They aggravate you, manipulate you, frustrate you, dominate you, pester you ... and on and on. Yet still you know that Christ has put it within you to extend *radar love* to them.

Sometimes I think God places people on my radar screen just to give me a reminder of where I stand on this love issue and show me where I have considerable room for improvement. I like to think of these people as "Heavenly sand paper!" God has a way of using them to expose and smooth out the rough spots in my life.

One area I know God uses as a barometer for what's really inside me is traffic. It's sad, but true that I can tell immediately when I get behind the wheel of my car whether I'm living in the Spirit or not. Something about that four-wheel-drive just brings it out of me and reveals what's *real*.

I was wanting to turn right on red not too long ago when I approached a major intersection in my area. Because I was the second car at the light, I didn't have quite enough room to squeeze by the car in front of me and be on my merry way. This particular traffic light is known to be the longest in the world—er, maybe the longest in *town*—so I had no intention of sitting through the entire cycle when it was just a matter of inches preventing me from making my turn. I inched up and inched up some more, hoping the lady in front of me would catch a glimpse in her rearview mirror and scootch up just a little bit more to accommodate my anxious lead foot.

> **Sometimes I think God places people on my radar screen just to give me a reminder of where I stand on this love issue and show me where I have considerable room for improvement.**

Inch ... Inch-Inch ... Inch-Inch-Inch ... *"C'mon lady!"* I bellowed in my empty car. "Why-I-oughta….."

And then the testosterone kicked in. I shifted into four-wheel-drive mode, tackled the ditch to my right, and came up right alongside the lady, who I imagined to be intentionally holding me up. Man, I was ready to give her one of those "you-know-what-I-think-of-you" looks!

But you know what? She didn't have a clue—not the faintest idea that I had gone from zero to sixty on the anger scale just because she hadn't seen me and didn't realize I had wanted her to scoot up and put herself closer to the oncoming traffic. Man, I had been a Class-A jerk to this totally unsuspecting lady, and then it was as if the Holy Spirit tapped me on the shoulder to remind me that Christ had died for her too. "I know, Lord," I said aloud. "How could I have ever thought for a moment that she was any less important than me?"

My litmus test for authentically showing *radar love* is traffic. What's yours?

Misguided Love

Sometimes we may mean for our love for others to be like *radar love*, but if we're not completely focused upon Christ, it becomes *misguided love*. There are several examples of *misguided love* that immediately come to mind: *radar-detector love, memory-lapse love,* and *Milton-Bradley® love*. Let me explain.

Radar-detector Love

When we practice *radar-detector love*, we cruise through our daily schedules with something akin to a spiritual radar detector planted firmly against our forehead. We'll be going about our business, stopping for gas, picking up groceries, dropping kids off at practice and suddenly … beep … beep … beep. Before we even realize we're doing it, we've shifted gears and we're nothing but sunshine and rainbows as we greet the pastor at the carwash. "Why, yes, Brother John, it *is* a blessed day. And yes, we are so blessed to be able to enjoy it. Blessed, blessed, blessed—that's what I *always* say!" Out of nowhere, our *radar-detector love* has transformed us into a model Christ-follower.

The problem with radar detectors is that they're made for people intending to break the law. Doubt that? If you weren't planning on regularly breaking the law by speeding, why else would you need a radar detector? To know where all the good donut shops were? I don't think so.

Though it's hard to 'fess up to, for those of us who occasionally strap on the ol' radar detector, it just simply means that we're only on the lookout for other Christ-followers, people we know to be believers that we're concerned with acting "right" around. What we're saying in effect is, "If I don't know you and you're not a Christ-follower, I don't have to be on my best behavior and living like Christ." Harsh, but uncomfortably true.

Memory-lapse Love

We've all experienced *memory-lapse love* if we've been a Christ-follower for more than a few months. Some of us suffer from a chronic case of it; others just have an occasional flare-up. When you fall victim to *memory-lapse love,* you resemble a match that has just been struck. You flare up with incredibly intense white-hot heat but then, so very quickly, you go from burning bright to burning out. You may have just heard a particularly inspiring Sunday sermon and leave church on fire for Jesus. Maybe your weekly Bible study lesson was especially relevant for you and you can't wait to share your insights with those outside the group. Maybe you've even been on a mission trip and returned home intent on remembering the suffering you've seen and doing everything you can to help the people you left behind. It could be these or any number of similar settings in which you temporarily feel motivated and inspired to "be Jesus" and to "make a difference," but your focus loses its intensity once "real life" creeps back into your days. Your intentions are genuine at the time, but they evaporate against the demands of your job, your family, and other so-called obligations. *Memory-lapse love* is definitely a treatable condition, but one that requires a committed course of treatment that few see through to completion.

Bill Cosby used to do a funny bit in his comedy routine. Knowing he would get universal understanding, he would ask his audiences, "Have you ever been sitting in the living room and think you need to go get something out of the kitchen, but when you get to the kitchen you forgot what you went in there for?"

"So you leave the kitchen, go back to the living room, and just as you're about to sit down, you remember what you were going for." It was here he would pause for the comedic effect before continuing, "Now, I would suggest that if you want to shorten that process, just grab your bottom and give it a good squeeze and it will simulate the experience of sitting back down in the chair!" It's a funny visual, but the comedy master makes a good point!

For those of us who suffer from the symptoms of *memory-lapse love,* I think we need more than a squeeze in the bottom. I think maybe a good solid kick in the pants would do an excellent job of reminding us that *radar love* is the objective, and it's worth remembering!

Milton-Bradley® Love

This type of love is for people who know all the rules of the game. They know when to pass go and collect $200, and they know all too well how to play, but they're losing on the inside. They are able to fool even their closest of friends because they've become professional game-players. They pepper their conversations with just the right words that show at least some mastery of the life they're appearing to lead. They show up when and where they're "supposed" to and roll the dice when it's their turn. They've even got a strategy to their game-playing techniques. Sadly, when the game ends, so does their commitment to a Christ-honoring lifestyle.

The "Love" Chapter

It's a rare wedding that we go to that we don't hear or read some reference to 1 Corinthians 13 either during the ceremony or in the program. It's overused and has lost some of its bang for the buck, as far as I'm concerned. Don't get me wrong—it truly is the love chapter of the Bible and describes love how it is to be in its most Christ-like manner. It's our familiarity with the words that has watered down its significant meaning. Most of us could probably recite the better part of it by heart. "Love is patient, love is kind. I wonder what the score is on the Cowboys' game." I'm probably the only one who's *ever* done that during a wedding ceremony—*not!*

I recently did a little "adjustment" to this chapter to see if my thoughts on *radar love* stood up against the definitive explanation of love. Before I share my "Draper Translation," you must know I don't seriously endorse altering the inspired word of God. This was merely a challenge to see if *radar love* measured up to God's definition. Within verses 4–8a and verse 13, wherever I saw the word "love" I simply substituted *radar love* in its place to see if it stood true:

> Radar love is patient, radar love is kind. It does not envy, it does not boast, it is not proud. It is not rude, it is not self-seeking. It is not easily angered, it keeps no record of wrongs. Radar love does not delight in evil but rejoices with the truth. It always protects, always trusts, always hopes, always perseveres. Radar love never fails ... And now these three remain: faith, hope, and radar love. But the greatest of these is radar love.

Okay, I'll be the first to admit it sounds a bit unconventional. But if you look back at all we've said *radar love* is, does, and stands for, it seems to me that *radar love* is a good fit in "the love chapter."

The Rest of the Story ...

By now you're probably wondering whatever became of the girl on the porch who shot herself. She lived and made a full recovery—at least physically. We stayed in touch with her in the weeks following her hospital stay. We bought her a Bible, shared the good news of Christ with her, and invited her to church with us.

When she met us for church, she showed up in what I would guess to have been her best dress. It was colorful, considerably revealing, and cut very low in the front. It was the kind of dress that most people would expect to see at a disco, not Sunday morning church. We knew her intentions were to come for worship, yet could feel the disapproving stares from much of the congregation.

"How could she wear *that?*"

"Why would you bring someone like *that* to church?"

"Doesn't she know what's appropriate for church?"

I was sad for her and mad at the judging masses. I also realized something that morning as I watched our friend be charged, tried, and found guilty in a silent trial by those who considered themselves to be anything but her peers. In just a matter of moments, I saw how many of us reserve our *radar love* for those within our protective walls of our respective churches. We share it with those we consider to be *safe* and *worthy,* those we're confident that will receive it and express the appropriate appreciation for our actions. We're checking the boxes, so to speak; we're just not winning any souls to the Lord in the process.

If the task of showing *radar love* to your neighbor is too overwhelming to fully embrace, and you doubt your abilities to always "be Jesus" to others, let me offer two suggestions: 1) *Always* remember this is a cooperative effort between you and the Holy Spirit living in and through you. This is not a solo effort. You are right to assume that you can't do this alone. Your only hope for success is to allow the Holy Spirit to guide you on a moment-by-moment basis; and 2) Take comfort in knowing that we're not responsible for our neighbors deciding to follow Christ; we're only responsible for telling them *how* to follow Christ. After that, the direction of their heart and their eternal destination is out of our hands and in that of the Holy Spirit.

Just remember, boys and girls, that Mister Rogers' neighborhood is nothing more than some cardboard props, a few goofy-talking hand puppets, and takes place on a sound stage.

And our neighbors are all around us.

For bonus content related to this chapter, please visit:
http://www.happytodoit.jlog.com

5

A 'COUNT' ABILITY

Several years ago Elizabeth and I went to visit some friends who lived well past the outskirts of town. As it had been a while since our last visit, we had to call and get directions once we exited the interstate onto the two-lane farm-to-market road leading away from the city. Normally we would rely on the smooth-talking, even-tempered lady who lives inside our little GPS box in the console, but this was so far out in the middle of nowhere, even *she* didn't know where we were headed!

I called our friends and started relaying the directions to Elizabeth to write down as we continued driving past the edge of civilization. "Okay, past the tree that looks like it was struck by lightning ... left at the white picket fence ... right at the third gravel road you come to ... and you'll be 7/10ths of a mile down the road ... what's that? *We can't miss it!?*" Sure enough, our friends' directions were exactly correct. What they lacked in measurable precision, they made up for in descriptive adjectives!

Once at their gate, however, the *real* navigating began. Two full-grown and incredibly intense Dobermans raced to greet us. Did I mention they were *intense?* That's kind of like saying Wiley Coyote is persistent! And did I say *greet?* Maybe *greet* is putting it a bit too friendly.

I meant to say *eat!* Fangs bared, eyes bugged out, and barking like we were from Animal Control. These "boys" were large and in charge and wanted to make sure we knew it!

As our friends came to claim the dogs and return them to their pen, Elizabeth and I finally felt comfortable enough to step *out* of the car. We were loaded with gifts and food and were just beginning to make our way across the yard when our two canine "friends" broke loose and headed straight for us. The deviled eggs went flying, Easter baskets became collateral damage, and Elizabeth and I ran faster than we've *ever* run in our entire lives toward the front door! I never knew our middle-aged bodies could hoof it so fast! It couldn't have been our ability alone. It *had* to be *super*natural ability.

We've since laughed at how funny we must have looked, high-tailing it around the flowerbeds, up the porch steps, and through the front door. We've imagined that, had the front door not opened so easily, there would have been a Randy-and-Elizabeth-shaped cutout in the screen door! Realizing how fast we moved when we *had* to hustle got me to thinking about what other skills, talents, and abilities I have that I had let lie dormant and unused; the ones I only called up for service when I *had* to.

Just like my race across my friends' yard was changed from a natural, God-given ability into a *super*natural, adrenalin-charged sprint, I soon realized that I had lots of other God-given abilities that could be transformed into much more than I was currently allowing them to be used for. If I was *intentional* in turning over my talents to God for *His* purposes ... my mind began to consider the possibilities. The story in Matthew 25 of the Master and his servants immediately came to mind. Just before going on a lengthy journey out of the country, this man called three of his servants to meet with him. To one he gave five talents, to the second he gave two, and to the last he gave but one.

While their Master was away, the first servant put his money to work and doubled his investment. The second servant did likewise. But the third servant, fearful of losing his one and only talent, dug a hole and buried it until his master's return. Anxious to see the return on his investments with his servants, the Master called them to his chambers immediately upon return. The first servant stepped forward and said, "Master, you entrusted me with five talents. See, I have gained five more" (v. 20).

The master replied, "Well done, good and faithful servant! You have been faithful with a few things; I will put you in charge of many things. Come and share your master's happiness!" (v. 21). The same scene played out for the second servant as he, too, was invited to share in his master's prosperity. When the third servant shared his investment strategy with the master, he was met with the wealthy man's wrath. "You wicked, lazy servant ... You should have put my money on deposit with the bankers, so that when I returned I would have received it back with interest. Take the talent from him and give it to the one who has ten talents. For everyone who has will be given more, and he will have an abundance. Whoever does not have, even what he has will be taken from him. And throw that worthless servant outside, into the darkness, where there will be weeping and gnashing of teeth" (v. 26–30).

> **We are to take what we've been blessed with, invest it in others, and receive a bounty of other abilities such that we never exhaust our gifts and stand to transform them into supernatural talents with each God-inspired use of them.**

Can you see the extreme importance God places on us using the abilities and resources He gives us? We're not to sit idly by, fearful of losing what He has given us. Nothing could be further from the truth. No, we are to take what we've been blessed with, invest it in others, and receive a bounty of other abilities such that we *never* exhaust our gifts and stand to transform them into *super*natural talents with each God-inspired use of them.

There's nothing God cares more about than His children—those who already know and love Him and those who have yet to hear of His saving grace. In a cycle that knows no end, God uses the skills, talents, and abilities of those who know and love Him and transforms our gifts into *super*natural abilities to reach those who haven't yet come into His fold. It's the ultimate gift that keeps on giving!

While we each have a combination of talents and gifts that is unique to us, I believe there are three primary abilities the Lord has given to all believers: response-ability, x-spend-ability, and assess-ability. Mix these three universal gifts with our special blend of God-given talents, and each of us is gifted in a way to touch others for Christ that *no one else in the entire world*—past, present, or future—can ever duplicate. Just as our fingerprints are ours alone, so also is the composite of our skills and talents. There is, however, one universal trait they all share, and that is they were given to us to enlarge Christ's kingdom during our brief stay on earth.

Response-ability

Did you know there is a significant difference between *responding* to a comment or a set of circumstances and *reacting* to it? Though we often use the two words interchangeably, there is a profound difference between the two, and it can literally affect where someone spends eternity. Let me explain: a reaction is usually more of a knee-jerk reflex, and it happens without thought; a response is a thought-out and planned reply. One is instinctive in our natural state; one is inspired in our spiritual state. One has the ability to hurt, offend, and harm others; the other has the potential to relieve guilt and worry, calm fears, and bring comfort. One is the generally accepted, way-of-the-world reply; the other is possible through a closely aligned walk with Jesus and a heart receptive to the Holy Spirit's influence. In short, when we react, it is our natural ability on display; when we respond, it is God's *super*natural ability being revealed.

Consider a few real-life scenarios and consider how you might speak and act in them.

The waitress is juggling too many tables, she brings out the wrong dressing on your salad, and your steak is undercooked. Do you *react* or *respond?*

Bumper-to-bumper traffic on the commute home, and just as you're about to switch lanes for the exit toward home, a guy in a half-ton pick-up cuts you off and makes you miss your exit. Do you *react* or *respond?*

You tell a friend about the outfit you're considering getting for the upcoming community gala. When you return to buy the dress, it's gone and later that evening at the event you see your friend in *your* outfit. Do you *react* or *respond?*

Generally, I don't like to make universal, there's-never-an-exception blanket statements, especially when it concerns people other than myself, but I'm willing to go out on a limb for this one: God would *always* prefer we *respond* rather than *react* in our dealings with other people. He would *always* prefer a reply that was thought out and one that takes into consideration the potential our words and actions have to bring someone *closer* to Him rather than *farther* away. When we stop to consider that every encounter we have with others has the potential to bring them closer to Christ, *responding* wins out over *reacting* every time.

Because He walked among men and encountered many of the same challenges we still face today, Jesus knew it wouldn't always be easy to respond to unbelievers rather than react. The New Testament is filled with examples of responses we are to emulate if we are serious about walking and living as Christ did. These kinds of responses include: a loving response, a praying response, a forgiving response, an encouraging response, and a serving response.

A Loving Response

If you read Jesus' directions about how to deal with others in Luke 6:35–36, you realize that Jesus had more than just a passing knowledge of dealing with contentious people, and yet see how He tells us to *respond* to them: "But love your enemies, do good to them, and lend to them without expecting to get anything back. Then your reward will be great, and you will be sons of the Most High, because he is kind to the ungrateful and wicked. Be merciful, just as your Father is merciful."

Think about a person in your life who just grates against your nerves. Maybe there are several people who you'd be fine if you never saw or heard from again—as long as you live! It's these exact people the Lord wants us to respond to in a loving manner. They're cantankerous, ornery, and like nothing more than to stir up that hornet's nest of emotions you associate with them. These are the precise ones Jesus would have you respond to in love.

A Praying Response

I know what you're probably thinking now. You're thinking, "I can fake the 'love thing' when I'm responding in front of others, but there's nooooo way I'm sending up prayers on behalf of those jerks at the office or those gossip mongers in the service league." You need to remember throughout this whole *react vs. respond* discussion that the only thing that matters to Christ is your heart in the matter—not how it appears to others, not what other people hear from your mouth or how gracious you seem to deal with others. It's impossible to offer a praying response to others without your heart genuinely engaged.

Matthew 5:44–48 challenges the prayer response for committed believers and discounts efforts of loving those "easy" to love: "Love your enemies and pray for those who persecute you, that you may be sons of your Father in Heaven. He causes his sun to rise on the evil and the good, and sends rain on the righteous and unrighteous. If you love those who love you, what reward will you get? Are not even the tax collectors doing that? And if you greet only your brothers, what are you doing more than others? Do not even pagans do that? Be perfect, therefore, as your Heavenly Father is perfect." So much for taking the easy way out on the prayer response!

I was battling some treacherous rush-hour traffic the other day. It was a Friday afternoon and people were wanting to be home *now*. I was traveling down the primary interstate that borders the northern end of the Dallas/Ft. Worth International Airport, and there were fender benders in both the east and west bound lanes. It was a sort of "perfect storm" setting for what my New Age friends might call "bad car karma."

Drivers were jockeying for spots in whichever was the fastest moving lane at the moment, all the while trying to rubberneck at the poor ol' sons-of-gun pulled over trading insurance information with another poor ol' son-of-a-gun! I was just as guilty, but had to pull my focus in, as I needed to get over *just one more lane* before the upcoming split. I signaled my intent and begin moving toward the left lane when … HHHHHHOOOOOONNNNNNKKK! Whoa, man! Where'd that guy come from? I jerked at my wheel, regained my place in my lane, and watched as the guy pulled up alongside of me to wave—with *one* finger!

Why I oughta … I thought to myself as he pulled ahead. And then, in a moment of *super*natural intervention, I felt impressed to pray for that guy. It *had* to be the Holy Spirit stepping forward in me, because my fleshly side wanted to do *anything* but pray for the guy who clearly didn't realize you wave with *all five* fingers, not just one!

So I'm still creeping along in traffic, convicted to pray, and I realize I don't have any idea what's going on in that guy's life. Maybe his wife just left him. Maybe his job is in danger. Maybe somebody kicked his cat off the front porch and he's still angry about it. Whatever it was, I didn't know the details, and it wouldn't have mattered if I did. My commandment was to *respond* in prayer. It wasn't my first reaction, and it wasn't easy at first, but I was just a few words into my prayer and next thing I knew, I was the one receiving the blessing. I had an opportunity to do just what Jesus said to do: "pray for those who curse you." I'm living proof it's a Christ-honoring, fail-proof system.

A Forgiving Response

Of all the responses Jesus wants us to have, I sometimes think the forgiving response is the most difficult, and yet it is a tremendous victory for the devil if we don't extend forgiveness to those who have hurt and offended us. Do whatever it takes to keep the devil from stealing the joy that God wants to give you when you offer forgiveness to someone who doesn't deserve it. Otherwise, you'll not only miss out on a blessing you could have received, but you'll not receive the forgiveness you so desperately desire.

> **Do whatever it takes to keep the devil from stealing the joy that God wants to give you when you offer forgiveness to someone who doesn't deserve it.**

Matthew 6:14–15 explains this basic principle of God's law: "For if you forgive men when they sin against you, your Heavenly Father will also forgive you. But if you do not forgive men their sins your Father will not forgive your sins." In the simplest of terms, this means if you're forgiv*ing*, then you're forgiv*en;* if you're unforgiv*ing*, then you're unforgiv*en*. I seem to have enough challenges in my daily life without passing up the gift of undeserved, yet completely free, forgiveness from our Heavenly Father. I don't want to do anything to stand in the way of the forgiveness that Christ wants to give.

An Encouraging Response

To encourage someone means to literally place courage *into* another person. If you trace the word "encouragement" all the way back to its Greek origins, it means to place courage into another person *on purpose*. Isn't that a great visual to remember whenever we have the opportunity to speak words of support into someone's life? Just picture yourself with a great big box labeled "courage" and you're pouring it a little bit at a time into your friend in need. It's kind of like filling up your car at the gas pump except you're topping off their tank with words of support, inspiration, and motivation.

We encounter people in need of encouragement every day and we have a choice to make. We can either be cheerleaders or jeer-leaders. We can intentionally speak encouragement into people's lives or we can criticize, condemn, and discourage them. It's a safe bet that Christ would have us take on the role of cheerleader over jeer-leader.

A Serving Response

This is the response that goes directly against our basic instincts and cultural norms because it tells us that to be first, we've got to be last. If this doesn't seem to make sense to you at first, you're not alone. Even back when the disciples were in the very presence of the Lord, they took to arguing about who among them would be the biggest, baddest one in the kingdom of God. Can't you just imagine what Jesus was thinking when He heard these men discussing who was most deserving to sit at His right hand in Heaven?

"I fed and watered His donkey at every little town this side of Nazareth," claims one.

"Yeah? Well I washed everyone's robes in the River Jordan," says another.

"That's nothing," says a third one. "I'm his half-brother!"

And to think, these guys were supposed to be the most devoted of Christ's followers. They were the hand-picked ones to carry the gospel throughout the world when Jesus was gone. The more you study the disciples, the more you realize that they were just like you and me. To their immense credit, they had literally walked away from their families and livelihoods to follow Christ, but that doesn't mean they made the trip without any baggage. Because they were fully human, they suffered from the same issues we all have at one time in our life. They were self-centered and totally insecure. They had doubts, fears, and lots of questions about what it meant to be a Christ-follower. Sound uncomfortably familiar? Though I'm not especially proud to admit it, it sounds a lot like me on any given day!

The cool thing about how Jesus dealt with this rag-tag bunch of twenty-somethings was that He knew their weaknesses, their character flaws, and the worst of their personality shortcomings. He knew it, and He still had faith in them to change and become doers of the word. Among the last lesson He left with His disciples was the admonishment that to become a leader among men, they had to become a servant to men; they would be their most effective in influencing those around them if they would become the most humble. And just as had been the case with all the lessons He shared with the disciples, His actions mirrored His words in Luke 22:27 when He spoke at the Last Supper, "But I am among you as one who serves."

The last time Elizabeth and I were filling up with gas, we decided to take advantage of the car wash adjacent to the filling station. We were pulling out all the stops and living large. Yes sir, I was treating my wife to the De-Luxe wash, wax, and rinse. "Nothing but the best for the love of my life," I told her as we followed the large arrows painted on the pavement that led us to the car wash entrance. Little did I realize that while I was reveling in my moment as a thoughtful husband, moments later I would be given the opportunity to test drive my own advice about *responding* rather than *reacting*.

I tried punching the code on the bottom of the receipt into the beat-up keypad that triggered the wash to start. 7-5-6-9-enter. No water. *7-5-6-9-ENTER!* Still no water. One more time and still no soapy spray covering my car.

"Try that button to the left," said Elizabeth. "The one that says 'Press HERE for help.'"

"I did already. I think there must be something wrong because I *know* I didn't put the number in wrong *all three times!*"

Suddenly the speaker box came to life. "What you need?" it asked.

"I want a deluxe carwash."

"Press code in."

"I *did* 'press code in.'"

"Bring ticket here!"

So I backed out of the entrance and circled back around to the front and went in to meet Mr. Grump-in-the-Box. He was just as pleasant on the inside as he had been on the outside.

"Yeah, I'm the guy who …"

"What you need?"

"Well, what I want is …"

"You press code. Do you press code? You must press code."

I was getting nowhere fast, and I had two options as to how I was going to get there—all bent out of shape, mad, and frustrated or calm, chilled, and accepting. I chose the latter … with a serious dose of humor thrown in. I got to laughing on the inside and felt it welling up inside of me with every word this guy said. I got one more set of instructions and got out of the store before my sides split open from holding the laughter in. Elizabeth could see it coming, and we were both in tears and gasping for breath before we made it 'round back to try again. We got a great tagline that we still throw out to one another at the most unexpected times for a good laugh. To this day, when the kids buzz us on the intercom in our home or call us on our cell phone, we still occasionally answer, "What you need?" Of course with some attitude! (All fun intended!)

We eventually got the car washed, but we got a whole lot more than that. We got a chance to practice *responding* rather than *reacting*; to choose the high road over the low road. As believers, if we are to truly live a Christ-honoring life, we can't treat others with a 'what-you-need' attitude.

Instead, we would all do well to treat every encounter like the hundreds of home office associates at Premier Designs Inc. do *thousands* of times each business day. They respond like it's truly a privilege to meet your need. Think I'm kidding? Ask anyone associated with the company and they'll tell you it's one of the first things they learned from the founders, Andy and Joan Horner: that if they were to represent the company in *any* capacity, they were to greet each and *every* customer and jeweler with the offer to serve them. Whether it's a home jewelry show and you're placing an order or calling the company headquarters to return a broken earring, my bet is they'll offer up a genuine smile, look you squarely in the eye, and say, "How may I serve you?"

"How may I serve you?"

Can you imagine how this would change your little corner of the world if you viewed every exchange with someone else as the opportunity it is rather than the imposition we so often view it as? Try it for a day…then two and see if it doesn't rock your world in amazing ways.

So long, "what-you-need?" *reaction*.

Hello, "how-may-I-serve-you?" *response*.

X-spend-ability

Everybody has *spend*-ability—the ability to spend what we *have* on what we *want*. What separates each of us is the X factor or the unknown amount each of us has to spend. It's one of the last taboos of refined conversation—how much money you make, how much you've amassed, and how much you want others to think you have. People will talk about just about everything in business settings, amongst friends, and at holidays spent with long-lost family, but the one subject most people won't discuss is their *x-spend-ability*—how much they make and how they spend it.

I think it is because most people realize that how and where they spend their money is a direct reflection of what they consider to be the top priorities of their life. I've heard that if you want to see what's important to someone, just look at their day-timer or their daily schedule and you'll quickly see that they make time for what is most important to them. I completely agree but would add to that deductive line of thought to suggest a look at someone's checkbook register or monthly credit card statement, because there you will see what is of value to them.

Even before MasterCard and Visa ruled the universe and before there were ATM machines in just about every retail establishment throughout the world, Jesus knew that how we spend our money says more about us than our words ever can. It's the ultimate action speaking louder than words example. If you consider where your money goes, both for the "have-to" bills and the discretionary spending, it basically comes down to two primary avenues where your money can be allocated: on yourself or on others.

Jesus warned His followers not to concern themselves with spending much of their allotted days acquiring things that would eventually amount to nothing more than ashes and dust. He told His disciples clearly in Matthew 6:19–21 that their lives were better spent investing in people, not the things of this world, as He says, "Do not store up for yourselves treasures on earth, where moth and rust destroy, and where thieves break in and steal. But store up for yourselves treasures in Heaven, where moth and rust do not destroy, and where thieves do not break in and steal. For where your treasure is, there your heart will also be." He's telling them and us that whatever you *purchase* here on earth will eventually erode and fall apart, but what you *invest* in, namely relationships with others, are investments that can impact where someone spends eternity. Jesus challenges us to send our investment *ahead* of us rather than leaving it behind to gather dust. Make this command personal, and think of it in terms of your relationship with your spouse or kids. It becomes immediately clear where our investment is to be when viewed with this perspective. Ask yourself, would you rather leave your kids with the security of having grown up in a loving, Christ-honoring home and a relationship with Jesus, or would you rather leave them Grandma's silver service?

Beyond the welfare of your loved ones, Christ also commands us to spend our riches investing in our local church. He tells us in Luke 6:38

that however much we give, we stand to be given back considerably more. It may not be measured in dollar bills and stock shares, but the value of what Christ will give us in return for investing in our church is the highest yield we'll ever experience. Look at how He explains the payback plan of God: "Give, and it will be given to you. A good measure, pressed down, shaken together and running over, will be poured into your lap. For with the measure you use, it will be measured to you" (Luke 6:38). Give little; get little. Give big; get big. It's a biblical financial decision Wall Street will never get.

> **He tells us in Luke 6:38 that however much we give, we stand to be given back considerably more.**

Years ago when Elizabeth and I were facing the worst financial situation of our lives, we were tempted to file bankruptcy. We came close but resisted only after the Holy Spirit laid it upon my heart to honor my debts and repay everyone we owed in full. It was some rough sledding for a couple of years as we struggled to get by and began attacking our mountain of bills, but the Lord proved more faithful than we could have ever begun to imagine.

We had received a commission check from the previous month's business and applied it to every bill we could. There were still lots more creditors beating down our door, but we were making progress a little bit at a time. As the saying goes, for long stretches on end, we had "more month than money," but we were determined to see this through to the end. This particular month we had stretched the funds as far as they could go and were left with just the right amount for our tithe. The only problem was, my family had gotten used to lots of luxuries—luxuries like food, electricity, and a roof over their head.

What to do, what to do? Obviously common sense told me to use the money for the necessities and that God would surely understand. The insistent check in my spirit, however, told me it was all the Lord's in the first place, and at the very least, I needed to be faithful in my tithe. Convicted by the Holy Spirit, I wrote the check, and we left for Sunday services. When the offering plate was passed, I just couldn't bring myself to relinquish the check. The same thing happened later in the day during the evening services. The offering came and went, and I chose not to participate.

At that time in my life, my dad and I had the tradition to close up the church together on Sunday night before heading to their house for a big family dinner. We were walking back to his office when I reached into my coat pocket and released my check to God and His church. I knew that with the deposit of this check, our account would be zeroed out until the start of the next month.

"Dad? What I'm about to do is the greatest act of faith I believe I've ever made in my life," I said as I handed him my check.

My dad didn't miss a beat as he took the check from my hand and said, "Randy, you'll never regret this, because you can always trust God. He is faithful to do what He said He would do."

The next day I received an invitation to come and visit with a gentleman who was starting a new business and wanted to ask me some questions about the new direct sales company I had recently joined. I didn't know everything about my new company, but I was enthusiastic and more than happy to share what I had learned so far.

We visited for a couple of hours, and he asked if I could return Saturday morning to share much of what we had just discussed with his board of directors. Ironically, he thought it would make a greater impact coming from me directly than if he were to just repeat our conversation. I was "Happy to Do It" but couldn't help but wonder if they would really value my opinion so much if they were to see my bank statement!

Still, I showed up Saturday and told them everything I knew about direct sales *and then some!* They seemed receptive enough and appreciative for my limited insights, and just as I stood to leave, one of the men stood also to speak for the group.

"Randy," he began, "we appreciate you taking the time to come and share with us today, and we would like to pay you for your efforts."

That's a nice gesture, I thought to myself. *Totally unexpected and totally unnecessary, but still very considerate of them.* I'm imagining maybe $25 or a gift card to a restaurant or heck, maybe even coupons for a couple of Happy Meals! Anything was over and above what I was expecting.

The gentleman interrupted my thoughts and continued, "So, if it's all right with you, we'd like to write you a check for $5,000."

I couldn't help myself at that moment as tears seemed to come from nowhere and began trailing down my cheeks. I couldn't even speak at first. All I could do was think of my dad's words when I handed over my check, "Randy, you can trust God. You'll never regret it."

> **Give with the excitement that you're spending God's money on God's causes for God's people.**

Don't misunderstand my point here. I am in no way telling you that if you empty your bank account, God will miraculously fill it back up in a week's time. He might. He certainly can. But don't give with that expectation. Give with the excitement that you're spending God's money on God's causes for God's people. Give what you can with the exciting belief that God can take the resources He's entrusted you with to bring about life-changing experiences of those He wants you to impact. Faithful obedience is the issue here; money is just an incidental.

The wealthiest woman I ever met was also among the godliest women I've ever known. Her name was Mary Crowley, and she used her money to do more good than most people think possible in a lifetime. She started a company called Home Interiors and Gifts, and over the course of her lifetime, the company thrived, earning tens of millions of dollars in revenue. As a testimony to God's never-ending resources and the blessings He gives to those who give to others, Mary wore a necklace with two small shovels hanging from it. One shovel was smaller than the other and about the size you'd find on a charm bracelet, and the larger one was precisely twice as big as the little one.

I never saw Mary without the shovels necklace and used to watch her light up when someone would ask the significance of them. Her eyes would sparkle as she began to explain, "Well, the small shovel is mine and the big shovel is God's. I shovel all I can out as fast as I can and He shovels it back in with His shovel as fast as he can. You just can't outgive God. It's not possible."

Assess-ability

God gives each of us *assess-ability* because He wants us to know in advance that He will make the final assessment on our lives, but if we know it's coming, we can live a life in preparation for that moment when we stand before Him. It's like a teacher who gives you a very detailed study outline and tells you *exactly* what will be on the test. That way, there is no excuse for not doing well when test day arrives. The biggest difference between, say, a high school chemistry test and this test of a lifetime is that these results really will go on your permanent record—*permanently.*

Just as a teacher or coach equips you with knowledge and skills and holds you accountable to know and use them, God has also given us our own unique blend of skills and abilities, and He promises there will be a final *assess*-ment. It is the wise and righteously fearful believer who will pay attention to the details of the coming *assess*-ment and realize it is through our works and words that we can be best prepared for the comprehensive final exam of our lives.

We can find some "study clues" about God's view of our works by reading 1 Corinthians 3:12–15 "If any man builds … his work will be shown for what it is, because the Day will bring it to light. It will be revealed with fire, and the first will test the quality of each man's work. If what he has built survives, he will receive his reward. If it is burned up, he will suffer loss; he himself will be saved, but only as one escaping through the flames."

God is telling us that whatever we give our time to, however we get the job done, and whoever we impact along the way will be judged when we stand before Jesus in Heaven. Wherever you earn your living, God has placed you there to make an impact on those around you. Your *assess-ability* will be reviewed as Christ takes into account whether you were available to others or removed from them. Did you view your co-workers as an inconvenience and an insignificant part of your day, or did you see your interaction with them as opportunities to enrich their eventual and eternal destination? Be wise, and use your God-given *assess-ability* to evaluate your works and make them worthy of God's approval.

It won't just be our works that will stand judgment before Christ but also our words. Jesus gives us fair warning to be cautious and kind in our choice of words in Matthew 12:36–37: "But I tell you that men will have to give account on the day of judgment for every careless word they have spoken. For by your words, you will be acquitted, and by your words you will be condemned."

Our actions.

Our words.

Our judgment.

The good news is that we already know the test questions. We've got all the answers, too. Now all we have to do is practice a little personal *assess-ability* on ourselves. This course of study doesn't lend itself to "pulling an all-nighter" in hopes of filling our heads with some last-minute knowledge. It's also the type of study we'd do best to stay up on the daily reading because, taken too much at a time, the lessons are overwhelming and occasionally just short of believable. But if we stay with the "curriculum," take assignments as they come, and keep our hearts and minds trained upon the teacher, we'll make steady progress *upward*. And as challenges arise, and they surely will, if we honestly evaluate where we need to "study up," we stand a bit more ready to face the final test from our perfect teacher.

We don't have to look much beyond our friends and family to see how we've each been blessed with different combinations of natural skills, talents, and abilities. One friend may be extremely creative but couldn't balance a checkbook to save her life. Another might be so mechanically inclined that he's the "go-to" dad come science fair time. And yet another may be able to sell ice cubes to an Eskimo. Regardless of our obvious tendencies, we've all also been given three distinct abilities that God wants us to use to grow ourselves in His word as well as bring others to know Him. These three universal abilities as we've discussed are *response*-ability, *x-spend*-ability, and *assess*-ability. We've all got them; it's just a matter if we choose to use them because, just as a specific talent will wane without practice, so will these three God-given abilities we are to use for Christ's kingdom. It takes the old adage "use it or lose it" to a new level.

We've also got to have what I call "rottweiler determination" to remain committed to using our abilities even when we'd just prefer to ignore the issue, turn a blind eye or deaf ear to a call for help, or tell ourselves it's just not our place to get involved. Now I'm sure you're wondering where I learned such a highly scientific term as "rottweiler determination" (or RD, as us "professionals" like to call it!), and I have to confess—it comes from watching my loyal and lovable rottweiler Shasta. (who is now in "dog Heaven.")

Shasta was the most determined dog I have ever seen in my life. She simply would not take no for an answer. Her favorite game was to play "Chase the Laser." She didn't care who she played with—best friend or complete stranger. She just wanted *somebody* to play "laser" with her. If you came into our kitchen, she'd stop to nudge your leg and then go and sit by the drawer where we kept the laser pen light. She clearly knew what she wanted, and it was just a matter of time before she found a willing player.

All she wanted of someone—*anyone*—was for him or her to shine the light around the room so she could chase it. And let me tell you—

that dog could chase that light as fast as you could wiggle it! It might have been the laser pen light she was chasing or the emergency flashlight we kept in the pantry or the big one thousand-plus candlepower "man's" floodlight we kept in the garage; it didn't matter to Shasta. She just loved going after the light and having the light shine upon her.

As I was watching Shasta chase the light with all-out abandon, not letting anything get in her way, I suddenly realized that this is just what God wants of us: to go after His light with crazy, do-whatever-it-takes joy and enthusiasm, just like Shasta. The good news for us is that the light we are to pursue doesn't move, shift, or ever run low on batteries. It's the light of Jesus Christ, and we have all the skills, talents, and abilities we need to go after it with all the sold-out energies we possess. It's why we're here and eventually the day will come when God will hold us accountable. In the meantime, our responsibility is not to worry about the accountability, but to focus on making our God-given abilities *count.*

For bonus content related to this chapter, please visit:
http://www.happytodoit.jlog.com

6

THANKS GIVING

Why is it that for many of us we wait until the fourth Thursday of November to sit down and officially give thanks for friends and family? Doesn't the Lord bring forth blessings, provisions, and answered prayers *every* day of the year? Don't we, as "the land of the free and the home of the brave," have infinitely more to be thankful for than most others who inhabit the planet Earth? Isn't our *worst* day a whole lot better than many other people's *best?*

If you've experienced a fraction of the blessings I've had in my lifetime, you couldn't say "thank you" enough times in a hundred years. And yet, what is it that we most dwell on? Faults, problems, shortcomings—call them what you will—but the bottom line is that most of us allow our days to be spent focusing on what is *not*, rather than what *is*.

All the Lord wants of us as His sons and daughters of the faith is to be thankful *wherever* we find ourselves: *wherever* He's allowed our paths to go, with *whomever* we're in the company of, and *whatever* the circumstances that make up our respective lives. All the Lord wants of us is to be *thankful* for the infinite blessings we've received from Him. He makes this abundantly clear in two often-quoted verses: Ephesians 5:19–20 and 1 Thessalonians 5:18. First, in Ephesians, Paul is telling the Christ-followers to not just give thanks, but to do so *joyously*, even to the point of singing: "Sing and make music in your heart to the Lord, always giving thanks to God the Father for everything, in the name of our Lord Jesus Christ." In 1 Thessalonians 5:18, Paul, Silas, and Timothy urge those wanting to follow Christ to, "Give thanks in all circumstances, for this is God's will for you in Christ Jesus." Did you catch the qualifier in these verses? Oh, wait ... there is none. There's not even the hope of a loophole (as *your* circumstances must surely warrant!) with a vague, immeasurable quantifier like *sometimes, frequently, regularly.* In just three strokes of the pen, the Lord explains under what conditions we are to be thankful: A-L-L.

I heard a good story that seems to grow a bit more outlandish each time my uncle tells it, but it sure makes this point in a wildly imaginative way. Sam and Dolly had recently retired and decided to hit the open road without so much as a map, hotel reservations, or an itinerary. Footloose and free for the first time in many years, they stopped at the first tourist attraction they came to on the highway out of town—a wild animal park.

As they wound their way through the park, they enjoyed the antics of the lions, giraffes, and monkeys from the security of their sedan. As they rounded the last curve before exiting the park, they came across a bull elephant standing squarely in the middle of the road. As Sam inched closer and closer toward the mammoth pachyderm, Dolly was busy snapping away with the camera. Thirty minutes later, however, when the elephant still hadn't moved from his middle-of-the-road spot, Sam and Dolly grew frustrated. What had started out as a funny, out-of-the-ordinary adventure had grown stale. Sam and Dolly had their share of "up close and personal" moments with the elephant and were ready to get back to their open road adventure.

Eventually the elephant did move, but not exactly where they wanted. It seems the hood of Sam and Dolly's car was just the right height for an elephant's behind! The steel buckled beneath the considerable weight as the back tires raised slightly off the ground. Dolly feared for safety, Sam for insurance coverage. Moments later, their "guest" appeared rested and nonchalantly stood to his considerable feet as he headed for the feeding trough at the edge of the field.

Though a bit worse for the wear, Sam and Dolly head for the exit and the interstate in short order. They weren't on the highway more than ten minutes when Sam noticed flashing red and blue lights in his rearview mirror. As the trooper passed car after car behind Sam, it became obvious that Sam was his intended pursuit. Sam pulled over to the shoulder as the trooper came to a stop right behind him.

"Sir, please step out of your car," barked the officer. "We've had a hit-and-run in the area, and your car not only matches the description of the car, but you've got a significant dent in your front fender and hood."

Sam quickly gathered his wits and began to recount the saga of the bull elephant at the wild animal park. Though skeptical, the officer took a statement from Dolly and came to believe their story. As the officer released them, Sam's frustration over the banged-up car and the misplaced accusations had gotten the better of him, and he told Dolly he wanted to go home and call the whole trip off. Dolly, too, was a little miffed at the misadventures of the day and agreed to return home. Sensing Sam's despair, Dolly even offered to drive so Sam could sleep off a bit of his anger while stretched out in the backseat.

Forty miles from home, Dolly pulled into a rest stop and left Sam sleeping peacefully in the backseat. The backfire of Harleys from a motorcycle posse woke Sam, and he decided to take advantage of the rest stop as well. In the meantime, Dolly returned to the car, completely unaware of Sam's absence, and headed toward home. Moments later, Sam exited the restroom and realized Dolly had left him stranded ... alone ... with some rough-looking, leather-clad biker "boys."

As a cold sweat broke out on his brow, Sam spotted the state trooper he had "befriended" earlier in the day pulling in to the rest stop. "Officer, boy am I glad to see you!" Sam blurted out as his cycle buddies scrambled. "You're not going to believe this, but ..." and off he went, explaining his dire straits at the roadside rest stop.

"Hop on in," offered the trooper. "I'm headed back to the station in town and can drop you off on the way."

Because of his extensive knowledge of the back roads and shortcuts in the area, the officer made extremely fast time, and Sam ended up getting back home before Dolly. Imagining the look of surprise on her face when she pulled up to the house, Sam decided to go out and greet Dolly when he heard her coming down the street. Shocked and bewildered at the sight of Sam on the front porch, Dolly fumbled for the brakes, hit the accelerator by mistake, and smashed through the garage door and into the kitchen before coming to a complete stop.

Later that night in the still of the darkness, Sam and Dolly each played back the events of the day in their weary minds. "Will the insurance company take care of the elephant damage *and* the garage damage? How will they know the difference? How long will it take to have the kitchen repaired? How could so much bad luck come to two people in a single day?" And finally, the ever-present, "Why us?"

You know, despite Sam and Dolly's eventful day on the open road, the Lord expects the same of us as He did of them: to realize what we have to be thankful for and dwell on it. But beyond this, I think the Lord wants us to be totally sold out to this business of being thankful; to become full-throttle "thanks givers" who show our gratefulness, appreciation, and thankfulness through our lives to the point of impacting those around us by our words of honor.

Daunting? Definitely.
Worth it? You betcha!

> **I think the Lord wants us to be totally sold out to this business of being thankful; to become full-throttle "thanks givers" who show our gratefulness, appreciation, and thankfulness through our lives to the point of impacting those around us by our words of honor.**

Before I elaborate on some of the more outstanding traits I consider to be part of the *thanks giver* lifestyle, let me point out a few of the "also-rans" in the close-but-no-cigar realm of thankers.

Thanks Seekers

Thanks seekers are the people pleasers, oftentimes going to great lengths to be recognized by their friends, co-workers, and fellow volunteers just to receive a few words of affirmation from their fellow man. It's not the satisfaction of a job well done or a selfless service rendered that motivates them but rather the hope of a few spoken accolades (preferably in full earshot of others to hear!) that may or may not ever come their way. Consciously bringing honor and glory to God through their actions isn't even on their radar screen, and as such, the only praise they'll ever receive are but a few fleeting words from a fickle fellow man.

Not surprisingly, the Lord foreknew our human tendencies and warned us to stay mindful of our motivations when serving others. Matthew 6:1–2 addresses this chink in the human condition: "Be careful not to do your 'acts of righteousness' before men, to be seen by them. If you do, you will have no reward from your Father in Heaven. So when you give to the needy, do not announce it with trumpets … to be honored by men. I tell you the truth, they have received their reward in full."

He's telling us straight up: Don't be a *thanks seeker.* If you're looking for the praise of men, that's all the reward you'll receive.

Thanks Fakers

At one time or another, we've all probably been guilty of being *thanks fakers.* We know the right words to say, especially to our church friends, but inside, we're just not "feeling it." We can rattle off platitudes about blessings, but deep in our hearts, we know our words ring hollow. We know we should be thankful for the dependable "beater" car in the driveway, but can't help but notice all our friends' late model cars with all the bells and whistles. And yeah, we've got a roof over our head, but the worse-for-the-wear furniture that's made it through three toddlers (and forty-seven sippy cups) is too old to be considered stylish, but not quite old enough to be called "retro." So we "talk the talk," but aren't truly "walking the walk." We are like the Pharisees Jesus was referring to when He said they "honor me with their lips, but their hearts are far from me ..." (Matthew 15:8).

> **Don't just go through the motions, putting on a show of thanks. Own the praise or don't say it at all.**

Don't just go through the motions, putting on a show of thanks. Own the praise or don't say it at all. Don't dishonor the blessings of the Lord by being a *thanks faker*.

Thanks Whiners

We all know our fair share of *thanks whiners*. They're serving all right, but not without letting everyone they come in contact with know that it's not without substantial sacrifice on their part.

Ever heard a few comments similar to these?

"Man, it's hot out here directing traffic in the church parking lot, but *somebody's* got to do it!"

"This blood drive is taking sooooo much more of my time than I expected, but I'll manage to get dinner on the table *somehow*."

"I was at least expecting a handwritten thank-you note from the pastor after I dropped that big check in the offering plate. Guess it wasn't enough to get his attention."

Do you think any of these "acts of service" elicit the kind of soul-renewing revival that genuine service from the heart brings with it? Not on your life—literally. This makes me think of the kid forced to sit in "time out" for misbehaving. After much protest, he manages to get his seat in the chair but lets his mother know his true feelings, his true heart, if you will, about his actions when he mutters, "I'm sittin' on the *outside,* but I'm standin' on the *inside.*"

Again, the book of Matthew addresses those of us who occasionally are "standin' on the inside" when it tells us, "Let your light shine before men, that they may see your good deeds and praise your Father in Heaven" (Matthew 5:16). If you're giving, give joyfully. If you're serving, serve joyfully. If you're speaking, speak joyfully. Give, serve, and speak as unto the Lord, and be thankful you have the means and ability to do so. It's like that popular bumper sticker making the rounds that says, "No whiners allowed." Christ's family here on earth is faced with enough challenges on a daily basis without those of us who are able-bodied souls singing the "Poor Me" chorus. Don't give to get. Don't be a *thanks whiner.*

Thanks Takers

The bolder "first cousins" of the *thanks seekers* are *thanks takers.* Like the seekers, they're working for the recognition and approval of others, but unlike the seekers, they'll all but demand their moment in the spotlight.

They're loud.

They're proud.

They're arrogant.

They're downright hard to ignore!

"RRRRRRRRRRRip" goes their checkbook as they write a Sunday morning tithe check. It's not enough to drop the gift in the offering plate. No, these turkeys have got to march right up to the pastor after service and hand-deliver their oh-so-sacrificial gift. Nothing like letting everyone around you know that you're upping your tithe thanks to your big raise!

Or what about: "Yep, I about wore through three hammers just working on that Habitat for Humanity house last week. Just look at that window sill! Didn't think I still had it in me, but by golly, I managed to do a pretty fair job, if I do say so myself!"

Or maybe this one: "I would have liked to have joined ya'll at Starbucks, but by the time I got finished cleaning up from Vacation Bible School, it was just me and the janitor in the building. It was late all right, but I left that place spic 'n span!"

You know this type. Maybe you've even been this type at one time in the past. Take to heart the words of Paul in Philippians 2:3–4 and realize for a moment that there is joy to be had in placing others and their cares above your own: "Don't be selfish; don't try to impress others. Be humble, thinking of others as better than yourselves. Don't look out only for your own interests, but take an interest in others, too" (NLT). Whatever you do, don't be a *thanks taker*.

So now I've loaded you down with "what *not* to be" (usually not good psychology to lead with the negatives, but hang on and I'll make a strong finish, I promise!), let me share with you what I think are some of the more outstanding characteristics of *thanks givers*, those experienced souls who know that not everything necessarily works out the way we *want*, but for the *best* when we keep our eyes trained on Jesus.

Thanks Givers Have an Attitude of Gratitude

Probably the most discerning characteristic of *thanks givers* is that they've cultivated a thankful attitude. It's not that *thanks givers* have it any easier than the rest of us (and sometimes a lot worse!); they just

> **Probably the most discerning characteristic of *thanks givers* is that they've cultivated a thankful attitude.**

choose to be thankful for what *is,* instead of what is *not.* They're not ridiculously grateful for any and all circumstances that come their way (gosh, I sure am glad God gave me this problem!), they're just thankful for the blessings they do have and those yet to come—even from a life-threatening diagnosis.

Sadly, modern society has, by and large, developed an "ingratitude attitude" that not only tolerates but encourages discord and equates contentedness with "settling." (Do the commercial tag lines "You deserve a break today …" or "It's L'Oreal® and I'm worth it!" ring a bell?) I recently had one of those moments where the unsaved world and the Christian world collided. From my vantage point, it became painfully clear that oftentimes it's hard to discern who's living in which world. My real life "object lesson" played out in the World Wrestling Federation® (WWF) arena.

One of the WWF's most notorious bad boys is "Stone Cold" Steve Austin. His fans are so off-the-charts devoted and vocal in their support of him, it borders on cult-like. Through obscene language and vulgar gestures, Austin has taken the bad boy persona to a new level in mass entertainment venues. He's even gone so far as to alter one of the Bible's hallmark verses, John 3:16, and promote his views and abilities with his own perverted reference: Austin 3:16. He's got "Austin 3:16" on just about every kind of piece of promotional material available—T-shirts, hats, buttons, bumper stickers, back packs—you name it, and it's got "Austin 3:16" printed on it! As offensive as this is to Christ-followers, the marketing of this twisted reference has been wildly successful, an indication that much of society finds the perversion acceptable.

The irony of all this is that I got to meet Austin, and he's got to be one of the nicest guys I've ever met! He didn't slam me up against the wall like a rag doll or even try to put me in a "half-nelson" when we were introduced. Instead, he was friendly, approachable, and sincerely appreciative we had come to see his show. In real life, he was nothing like his on-stage persona, and then it dawned on me: this guy with two vastly different personalities was very similar to the way many Christians are today. When you meet many believers on a personal, one-on-one basis, they are seemingly kind and caring individuals. Yet when it's "showtime," be it at the office, at school, or out in the community, they become just like the rest of the world, complete with vulgar language, offensive actions, and an overall attitude of self-centeredness and anger toward the rest of the world. You might say they're members of the WCF (Worldly Christian Federation)—just acting "the part" like the rest of the world.

Jesus knew a few things about being in the world but not of the world. During His time on earth, Jews and Samaritans didn't mix well with one another, to put it mildly. Tolerance of each other was rare; hatred was more the norm. So when Jesus came across ten Samaritan men stricken with leprosy on His way to Jerusalem, the fact that He stopped was more than a bit unusual.

"Jesus, Master, have pity on us!" they cried from the roadside. And Jesus said to them, "Go, show yourselves to the priests" (Luke 17:13–14).

The men did as Jesus instructed and were healed, and yet, only one of the men had the graciousness to return to Jesus and thank Him for His mercy. Imagine being completely ostracized from your hometown due to a disease that literally destroyed your skin, coming across a stranger who provides direction for the healing process, becoming completely healed and relieved of both your physical and societal affliction, and *not* returning to say "thanks for the tip, man." That's what we in the South call an *ingrate!*

We can learn from these men about what *not* to do. We can also learn from Scripture about exactly what *to do*. Whatever the size of your home or apartment, whatever the make and model of your car ("beaters" included!), whatever other "things" you possess—Christ-followers have the ultimate gift and that is Christ Jesus. Second Corinthians 9:15 says, "Thanks be to God for his indescribable gift." The creator of the universe gave up His Son so that we wouldn't have to spend eternity in the fires of hell—you, me, and every other *completely undeserving,* wretched soul who has ever walked the face of the earth.

Seems to me a thank you is in order. Maybe even an attitude of gratitude.

Thanks Givers Respond in Obedience

If we really love Jesus as much as our loose lips claim, then this love should manifest itself in a life of obedience. By obedience I simply mean hearing God's word and acting accordingly. Jesus told His disciples that their love for Him boiled down to one thing: obedience. Twice in one chapter alone in the book of John, Jesus equates obedience with love.

Whoever has my commands and obeys them, he is the one who loves me… (John 14:21).

And:

Anyone who loves me will obey my teaching... (John 14:23).

As a parent, some of my most fulfilling moments were when my two boys were obedient to me or their mom. It wasn't always on the first time we asked … or the second … but by the third time, boy, they knew we meant business! Occasionally, they'd just try to mess with me and Elizabeth and do whatever we were asking on the first time. During those rare times, I swelled with pride and happiness! As they grew older, from time to time they didn't even need to be told what to do to be obedient—they just did it! You talk about "off the chain" happiness for a father! Don't you imagine our Heavenly Father rejoices when His children behave the same way with willing obedience without having to be reminded?

While a prisoner in jail, the apostle Paul had no idea of the innovations in temptation that would come centuries later, yet he knew even back then the importance of monitoring what thoughts and images filled one's mind. In a zealous appeal to early Christians, Paul directed his followers when he said, "We take captive every thought to make it obedient to Christ" (2 Corinthians 10:5). Since the days of the earliest apostles, temptation has been man's constant companion. Little has changed since those days except now we are able to receive our opportunities for dishonorable and thus thankless behavior via high definition airwaves, real-time streaming, and in some cases, three-dimensionally at the local movie theater. If the Lord has put it upon your conscience that your idea of entertainment is not honoring to your Savior, you are, in effect, choosing to not be obedient and consequently rejecting the love of Jesus if you keep doing it. Serious talk I realize, but this business of obedience is of eternal concern to the Lord.

Play it safe and go the obedience route. Genuine *thanks givers* respond in obedience.

Thanks Givers Display Confidence

It's not that *thanks givers* don't have reason to worry or cause for concern, because they undoubtedly do. The difference between *thanks givers* and others is that *thanks givers* have confidence—confidence in the Father, Son, and Holy Spirit to guide and direct them through the good, the bad, and you guessed it, the *ugly*. They know that when challenges come their way, as they surely do for us all, they've got more than just a knee-jerk of a human reaction to respond with, and it all goes back to their beliefs in the one true Christ.

Knowing they've got the "eternity gig" all taken care of, *thanks givers* are guided by their beliefs in God and His words in the Bible. These beliefs then temper what they think about, which, in turn, affects their attitude regarding a situation. From there, it's the attitude that downloads the directions that play out as actions. It's a simple cause and effect relationship rooted in one's beliefs that looks something like this:

Beliefs —» Thoughts —» Attitude —» Actions

Simply put, what you believe will determine your thoughts; your thoughts will determine your attitude; and your attitude will determine the actions you take.

I've seen many fellow Christians face difficult times and, in the midst of the crisis, they become frustrated and/or disappointed because they've forgotten *what* they believe and *in whom* they believe. If only they could call upon their beliefs, specifically their belief that God is in control, then they would realize that God is in control of *everything.* Toss that around in the ol' cranium next time you're not where you want to be or things aren't how you want them. It's amazing how just clinging to this simple truth that God is in control of everything seems to alleviate a considerable amount of unwarranted stress and in turn, improves your thoughts. And these improved thoughts … you guessed it, have a positive impact on your attitude, which amazingly end up reflecting your actions. And so the cycle goes.

Colossians 3:2–3 tells us, "Set your minds on things above, not on earthly things," and that by doing so and dying to ourselves, our "life is now hidden with Christ in God." The chapter goes on to tell us to "put to death" (v. 5) all the earthly, sin-tainted behavior of our lives before coming to know Christ since we are now under His coverage. Imagine if I were to take a writing pen to represent me and wrap it in paper to symbolize Christ's covering of me and my sins. If I then put the covered pen inside my Bible, which represents God, and closed it, I would be covered and then covered some more. This is just how it is in our relationship with Christ: He covers us, and then God covers our cover. That's insurance coverage of the eternal kind!

Think of a recent challenge or difficult time in your life. Ever wonder how that particular set of unfortunate circumstances came to land on the front doorstep to your life? Go back to the pen, paper, and Bible example and apply it to your life. Anything, and I'm talking *anything,* that's come into your life has first passed through the loving hands of God the Father and then Christ the Son before it ever touched down in your life. That being said, doesn't it stand to reason that whatever difficulty you may have faced in the past or may now be facing has been allowed into your life for a reason? It's a certainty that God isn't inflicting pain and turmoil in your life just to watch you squirm. If there's a challenge in your life, there's a purpose behind it and a lesson to be learned. Take my word for it—learn the lesson, be done with the dishonorable behavior, and claim the confidence of your life in Christ.

Christ's disciple, Peter, is a stellar example of someone able to do the unimaginable as long as he kept his eyes on Christ, but who failed miserably when he looked away. At the Lord's direction, Peter and the other disciples had set sail across a lake while Jesus remained on the shore a bit longer. When it came time for Jesus to rejoin His disciples, He walked on the water toward the men's boat.

The disciples were terribly frightened at the sight of a man walking on water, but were greatly comforted when Jesus identified Himself to them. Ever the skeptic, Peter said, "Lord, if it's you, tell me to come to you on the water" (Matthew 14:28). At the Lord's direction, Peter stepped out of the boat *onto* the lake and began walking toward the Lord. But when the winds picked up and Peter took his eyes from Jesus, he began to sink, crying out to Jesus, "Lord, save me!" (Matthew 14:30) and immediately Jesus stretched out His hand and caught him.

Isn't that a terrific word picture that illustrates just how it is for us when we stray from the Lord and cry out to Him and realize He's always there? That omnipresence in our lives, no matter the circumstances, provides us as Christ-followers with a confidence that, despite our best efforts to screw things up, the Lord stands "ready, willing, and able" to reach out and pull us out of the sinking waves of our own creation.

I'll let you in on a bad habit of mine: sometimes I can't wait to find out how a story ends and I'll flip to the back of the book to see how it all ends. Does the good guy win? Is the villain defeated? Does "happily ever after" really come to pass for the book's main characters? If you've claimed Christ as the savior of your life, the answers to all these questions is an emphatic *yes!*

You see, I've read "the book" and read and re-read the end chapters where it says that we as believers, whether dead or alive, will be caught up in the blink of an eye and ushered into the glory of the presence of the Lord to spend all of eternity with Him. We win, and for that, I'm

> **That omnipresence in our lives, no matter the circumstances, provides us as Christ-followers with a confidence that, despite our best efforts to screw things up, the Lord stands "ready, willing, and able" to reach out and pull us out of the sinking waves of our own creation.**

thankful. Confidently thankful. As the Cathedral Quartet sings it, "I've read the back of the book and we win!"

I was reminded of the sweet taste of victory at a recent high school football game. In Texas, Friday night high school football is a way of life, literally. Families move in and out of certain school districts, not because of outstanding academics and test scores, but because of the number of state championships on the books. A Friday night gridiron victory is a vicarious pleasure entire communities rehash all throughout the following week until the next match-up.

I'm the first to say that some people put too much emphasis on it, but you'll also find me yelling just as loud as everyone else if the ref makes a cock-eyed call against "our boys." That said, in a rare moment of contemplation about a recent game, I suddenly came to the realization that, in many ways, the Friday night turf battles are amazingly similar to real life. Let me explain what I mean. It was the last game before the play-offs, and the lead had volleyed back and forth between the two teams, which just happened to be cross-town rivals battling for bragging rights for the entire next year. My team, the Mustangs, held their opponent to the last minute before they allowed them to score a game-tying field goal.

The buzzer sounded, and the teams regrouped on the sidelines for overtime. This time our opponents held us up to the end as we moved the ball to the three-yard-line in preparation to kick a last-second field goal. We were already doing the victory dance in the stands when the unimaginable happened—the kick was blocked! My emotions went from exhilaration to disbelief and frustration in a matter of seconds.

It was the second overtime, and the opponent scored on the first possession. Immediately, my confidence in the 'stangs evaporated, and I started packing up our stuff. Fortunately for the hometown boys, *their* confidence remained intact, and they rallied to match their opponent's score. Again, the final buzzer sounded as the scoreboard was reset *one more time* for a third overtime!

By now, exhaustion was setting in amongst the players, and it became evident that the game was going to be settled by whoever could hold on the strongest and the longest. Ultimately, my Mustangs kicked a lengthy field goal to win, but not without first exhausting themselves, their coaches, and their maniac supporters (myself included!).

On the way to the parking lot, the Lord spoke to me and showed me the similarities between the game I had just experienced with a full range of emotions (first up and elated, then down and deflated, then up and ...) and in life. "Randy," the Lord spoke, "that game is a lot like everyday life. There are challenges and victories, good times and bad, big issues and little cares. The difference is that you don't have to go through the roller coaster of emotions on a daily basis that you did tonight because I've already fought the big battle and you win. Just live out your life based upon this confidence knowing you 'win' in the end." That's enough to make you want to be a *thanks giver*—a *confident thanks giver*.

Thanks Givers Love to Encourage

For earnest *thanks givers*, encouraging others is a natural by-product of their perspective; it's almost like they can't help but encourage others because their intense thankfulness spills over into every area of their life, and they just naturally want others to experience the same fulfillment. First Thessalonians 5:11 tells us, "Therefore encourage one another and build each other up ..." It's not enough just to *think* something positive about someone else. You've got to go the distance and *say or write* these words of affirmation one to another. Otherwise you're denying the other person the blessing of the encouragement, which, on some days, can make all the difference in the world.

For example, every now and then Elizabeth will ask, "Did you think I looked nice today?"

"Sure, honey, I told you that first thing this morning."

"No, you never mentioned it."

See what I'm talking about? A simple uplifting comment shared with someone can totally alter his or her day for the better, and all it "costs" you is the forethought to share a few words of encouragement. Don't be like those people who weep and wail at funerals, saying, "I just wished I'd said … I never told him how much I love him … I wished I'd told her how much she meant to me …" Do it now and don't deny someone the joy your spoken words of encouragement can bring.

> **A simple uplifting comment shared with someone can totally alter his or her day for the better, and all it "costs" you is the forethought to share a few words of encouragement.**

As texting and e-mail have become mainstream methods of communicating, the handwritten note has become a rarity, even for intimate correspondence between loved ones. Still, I want to encourage you to take the time to actually *write* (complete with paper and pen!) a note of encouragement to those in your circle of influence on a regular basis. I place so much value on handwritten notes of encouragement I've received through the years that I actually keep a file of notes marked "Encouragement" in my desk just for a tangible, hold-in-my-hand-and-re-read-a-thousand-times reference for those days when I question if I'm really making a difference in others' lives.

In turn, I've been convicted of writing notes of encouragement to others so that they'll have the same "hard copy" evidence that they can refer back to now and again. Before you play the "time card" ("Randy, there's no way I've got the time to write everyone I need to encourage"), think of it this way: if all you did was write one note of encouragement a week for a year, at the end of the year you would have blessed fifty-two people with an uplifting and encouraging message that they might not have received from anyone else in the world. The ripple effect of such a simple act is not even fathomable as you stop to consider the impact on the fifty-two people and in turn, their encouraging impact on others, and so on and so on. One note, exponential returns.

> " I thought of you today and appreciate you. "

What else? Try putting feet to your intentions of encouragement and meeting a need in someone's life. Maybe it's a single mother needing some free childcare occasionally. Maybe it's a meal to someone laid up with an injury or illness. Or maybe it's just dropping a plate of cookies off at someone's home or office as a means of telling them, "I thought of you today and appreciate you." Unexpected blessings like this will blow their socks off, and the memory of your kindness will last long past the last tuna casserole or cookie crumb. By ministering to and encouraging those in need, you're "being Jesus" to others, and that's as good as it gets.

As effective as speaking, writing, and doing for others is in terms of expressing encouragement, without a doubt the most God-honoring thing we can do one for another is to pray *with* and *for* others. Not too long ago I had the privilege of meeting with a woman who was interested in joining our company. As we talked, she shared that her husband had recently lost his job. With a newborn in the family, she was wrestling with the maternal feelings of wanting to be there full-time for her baby, but needing to provide income to keep the family afloat financially. Needless to say, it was an emotionally charged issue for her family.

As she finished sharing her story and as we finished sharing our opportunity with her, Elizabeth and I felt moved to ask if we could pray for her. She agreed, and we all went before the Lord, laying her concerns at His feet, petitioning His guidance, and praising His blessing of the new life in her family. As she stood to leave, we committed to continue to pray for her in the future that she could find more balance in her home/work life. Not long after we parted ways, I received a call from a the lady who had brought her to our home, calling to report the impact those few words of prayer offered up in a circle of four had on this woman. At twenty-seven years of age, this committed wife and mother had never had anyone offer to pray for her, to help her present her praises and her problems before the almighty Lord and to help her experience the unsurpassing comfort of knowing His mighty embrace. I'm telling you, right then and there, I committed to being bolder and more intentional in my offers to pray *with* and *for* others as a means of showing my encouragement to them.

It doesn't take much to "earn your stripes" as a *thanks giver* who encourages. A few words spoken or written, a much-needed act of service, or a heartfelt prayer offered up all have the power and potential to help others move from a time of despair, discouragement, and defeat to an optimistic, "maybe-I-can-do-this" mind-set. You'll never know, and more importantly, others will never know, if you don't make the effort or extend the offer to be the blessing to others.

William Borden—the Life of a True Thanks Giver

As heir to the Borden Dairy estate, William Borden was brought up in a life of privilege. Upon graduation from high school, Borden was already personally awarded millionaire status. As a further part of his graduation gift, young Borden was sent on a round-the-world trip throughout Asia, Europe, and the Middle East.

It was on this trip that Borden's heart became heavy for the many people in these countries that had yet to hear of the saving grace of

Jesus Christ. At the conclusion of his extensive trip, Borden committed to becoming a missionary and returning to these unreached souls for the sake of salvation. It was also at the end of this trip that he wrote on the last page of his Bible just two prophetic words about his experience: "No reserves."

After pursuing an undergraduate degree from Yale, he graduated with the highest of honors. Besides the ongoing offer to join the family business, Borden also received numerous offers from some of the country's top companies at the time. It seems "anyone who was anyone" in the business world wanted William Borden to join their company. Still focused upon his calling to the mission field, Borden rejected all offers and wrote two more words at the back of his Bible: "No retreat."

From Yale to Princeton Seminary, Borden studied theology as a final step in his preparation to become a missionary. Following this last graduation, Borden immediately boarded a ship bound for China that promised an opportunity to minister to the people of that country. En route, however, Borden contracted cerebral meningitis and died within a month.

Confused and angry that God would call one of His most intentional servants "home" while on his way to save others, Borden's family retrieved his precious Bible from among his possessions sent abroad. It was there that they realized Borden's life was not his own, but that it was a life honorably and sacrificially lived for the glory of the Lord, for under the words "No reserves" and "No retreat" were written Borden's final words: "No regrets."

If, in small measure, we can emulate Borden's "all-out, full throttle" life it is as a *thanks giver* to Christ for His inexplicable gift of eternal life. With this in our back pocket, isn't it ours to live with:

an attitude of gratitude,

a response of obedience,

a confidence in Christ,

and *a call to encourage?*

By embracing a thankfulness for whatever the Lord allows our way, we, too, can claim a life of *no reserves, no retreat, and no regrets.* Hallelujah!

For bonus content related to this chapter, please visit:
http://www.happytodoit.jlog.com

Happy to Do It

7

TOO BLESSED TO BE STRESSED

I know Stress.

We've worked and worried alongside one another off-and-on for the better part of my fifty-plus years. I'm not exactly saying we're good friends; I'm just saying that throughout my life there have been more times than I care to admit where Stress has come for what I thought would be a brief visit and ended up moving into the guest bedroom for an extended stay.

It's not like I actually *invite* Stress in. But somehow, when I'm *most* consumed with my mounting personal problems and *least* concerned with maintaining a growing relationship with Christ, that presumptuous "intruder" seems to appear, pull up a chair, and make himself comfortable right in the middle of my self-absorbed life! Don't get me wrong—I've got what most people would consider "legit" reasons to be stressed out, but I also know that stress is not a by-product of a healthy relationship with Christ.

More often than not, Stress isn't the only "visitor" when my walk with the Lord is left wanting. Frequently, when Stress shows up, he's soon joined by another troublesome traveler that takes up residence in my heart and mind.

"Stress … I'd like you to meet Guilt."

"Guilt, this is my companion Stress. I'm confident you both will complement each other tremendously."

Okay, so it's not like I extend a formal introduction between my all-too-frequent lifestyle companions, Stress and Guilt, but once they hook up, they get along terrifically. Usually whenever Stress and/or Guilt resurface in my life, it is in the slightest of ways in the beginnig—almost imperceptible, really. Sometimes it's almost like I *sense* Stress creeping into my consciousness, but I'm usually quick to dismiss it as the Mexican food I had for lunch or the restless sleep from the night before.

"Nah, not this time," I tell myself. "I've got all the plates spinning at the same time. You talk about a multi-tasking mastermind! I oughta be booked on Conan with skills like this. Oh wait … the one on the left is starting to wobble … now the big one in the middle … there goes the one in the far back …"

Hellllllll-lo Stress. Here, let me get your bags. You remember where your room is? That's right, third door on the left …

I told you. I know Stress.

I'm not alone in my intimate relationship with Stress and all the underlying causes of an overextended lifestyle. We're overworked and under-paid. We're over-budget and under-financed. We're overweight and grossly under-exercised. We're over-committed, out of balance, and out of control. We are, in a word, *stressed*.

> "We're overworked and under-paid. We're over-budget and under-financed."

We drive past the sprawling homes of our contemporaries and consider their owners to be both successful and blessed.

We take a picnic to the lake and watch the large boats glide through the water while we battle ants on the shoreline. Again, we consider those we see from afar to be successful and blessed.

Maybe we indulge in a bit of voyeuristic wishful thinking as we watch people at the big electronic stores buy whatever they want with seemingly little regard to the price, while we forage through the DVD bargain bin. They're probably friends with the guys out on the big boats on the lake, you assume. It would seem to follow that successful and blessed people would hang out with others just like them, not the "average Joes" or worse, the down-and-outers.

What we fail to realize in the middle of all our speculating about the lives and lifestyles of the apparently successful is that with such appearances usually comes incredible stress. For example, on the street with the spacious homes and the perfectly manicured lawns, there's a good chance six out of ten of those guys are treading water financially, just trying to keep their head above water and keep up with the successful lifestyle their family has come to expect. Of the six, two are probably the proud owners of interest-only bank loans and would lose money if they were to move anytime in the near future. Almost everyone on the street keeps a running balance on their credit cards, carries two or three car loans, and is concerned about paying for their kids' college. Doesn't seem quite so "successful" now, does it?

The few gray hairs I'll admit to have brought with them a few nuggets of wisdom. One of the first lessons I learned as I settled into adulthood was that for all the appearances of success, many of the people we consider to have "made it" are miserable. The houses, cars, boats, and other outward trappings are just that—trappings that have them held hostage to a lifestyle, a job, or expectations of others and stressed out to the max. The more successful they become in the eyes of the world, the more stress they take on until … something gives way.

The Voice of Experience

It was the mid-1980s, and I was riding high on the real estate boom in Texas. At the time I had a fair amount of discretionary income, and so, when the car of my childhood dreams became available, I couldn't resist. It was a candy-apple red 1981 Jaguar XJ6. I paid $16,800 for that beauty and even believed a friend when he convinced me it was an "appreciating asset."

"It'll be a great investment," he said. "You can drive it for a few years and sell it for *more* than you bought it for."

I couldn't help myself. I wanted that car so badly that, I believed my buddy's warped sense of financial reasoning hook, line, and sinker. Had I *ever* known a car to increase in value with age? That was *so* beside the point. By this time, emotion had won out over reason.

I took possession of that fine piece of machinery and had enjoyed scooting around town for all of three weeks when Elizabeth and I decided to take it on a longer adventure. We were due in Ardmore, Oklahoma, by 7:00 pm and so had left our home by 4:00 to avoid the rush hour traffic.

About a mile north of the Red River (the dividing line separating Texas from Oklahoma), a red warning light came on. "Oh my gosh! There's no oil in the car!" I shrieked. Smoke soon started curling out from under the hood and coming through the air conditioner vents *into* the car.

It took everything I had in me at the time, but I squelched my rising temptation to ask Elizabeth why *she* hadn't put oil in the car recently. Almost 10 years of marriage at that point had taught me a lot about responsibility as well as the wisdom of silence. So there we were—the car was fuming and I was fuming! Stress was literally pouring out of both of us!

I pulled over to the shoulder to let "Red Wonder" cool down. I killed the engine for a moment to let everything completely rest. Minutes later, the engine had cooled off all right—cooled to the point of being "stone cold," in fact, and wouldn't so much as turn over when I turned the key. I could feel the stress continue to build in me, but did my best impersonation of a "Christian husband" to my anxious wife.

"Honey, I think we need to start praying. It's almost dark, and we seem to be stranded away from anywhere or anyone," I said. We held hands and prayed out loud for the Lord to help us in our situation. At the end of our prayer, I tried turning the key once more and, *"Vroom! Vroom!* Houston—we have lift-off!"

Don't misunderstand me here—there was still smoke coming from the hood, and we had rolled down the windows to release the smoke coming through the vents, but we were moving and we *had* to be getting closer to civilization with every smoky mile we traveled. The next mile marker we passed said "Marietta—eleven miles," so we knew there would surely be a gas station at the exit.

> **I was "looking the part" in a nice home and candy-apple red Jag, but inside I was piling stress upon stress.**

We were haulin' it down the highway because I wanted to get as close to the exit as we could before the engine totally collapsed. We saw the exit sign and were just at the top of the exit ramp when flames burst out from under the hood. Not smoke, but *flames!* So long engine. All hydraulic power had short-circuited, and I was doing everything in my power to steer the suddenly-stiff steering column just enough to keep it on the road so we could coast down the hill and into the service station.

We made it to the station, and Elizabeth made a dash for the hose. I gathered our stuff, jumped out to help Elizabeth, and watched the car of my dreams—my investment!—go up in flames.

Stress was having a field day with me at that point in my life. Just like my car, I was empty and burned out, had been pushed (in reality, I had pushed myself!) beyond sensible limits, and was not operating as I was designed to operate. I was "looking the part" in a nice home and candy-apple red Jag, but inside I was piling stress upon stress. See what I mean about the outward "trappings" of success?

The latest statistic out of Washington, DC confirms what most of us have suspected all along: one out of one person will die. That's one of those statistics that doesn't even have any margin of error. No "plus or minus" 3 percent or 5 percent. These pollsters are bold enough to make the claim that they're 100 percent correct—all the time, every time. I think they must have read the article I saw recently in *USA Today*—"Can Living Kill You?" Ironically, the article urged readers to calm down and not panic over the inevitable!

How God Sees Stress

So now that I've filled you with enough happy thoughts to make you want to jump from the tallest bridge in town, let me share the best news you'll ever hear about stress: You, my friend, are simply too blessed to be stressed. Sure, there will always be challenging situations that present themselves in your life and you can be sure there's enough frustrating people to go around to bug, pester, and bother even the most easy-going among us. But by remembering just a few words of advice from the Bible, blessings are bountiful! We can keep our perspective intact and our blood pressure stable by hiding in our heart the words of our Lord.

Jeremiah 17:7 reminds us, "But blessed is the man who trusts in the Lord, whose confidence is in Him." It almost seems too simple, doesn't it? If all we're to do is trust in the Lord, we'll receive a blessing. It's a certainty that one day we will all die. It's also a certainty that when we place our trust in Christ, we not only have hope for today, but we're also given hope for eternity. It's like a spiritual "two-fer"—blessings for today and *forever*.

We can also receive the Lord's blessings by honoring Him with our lives. Psalm 119:2 says, "Blessed are they who keep his statutes and seek him with all their heart." Just because we know Christ doesn't mean we're consciously living a life worthy of His ultimate sacrifice. But when we choose *not* to live for Christ, we're the ones who are missing out. The good news is that *any*one at *any*time can change how they're living and begin to "seek Him with all their heart." The other good news is that when we do make this change, the blessings will soon follow.

My last example of how to move from a state of stressed to one of blessing is based upon Psalm 128:1, which says, "Blessed are all who fear the Lord, who walk in his ways." I share this one because for the longest time I misunderstood just what it meant, and I don't think I'm alone. I used to think it meant that if I strayed from doing what was right, even the slightest bit, God would look down and zap me with some type of spiritually-cosmic laser. Okay, it wouldn't really be a laser but could come in any number of ways—like an office place jerk or an unnecessary fender bender or an IRS audit. I knew instinctively that God could command "payback" from me at any time, and I lived in fear of it.

Fortunately I had a friend who shared a deeper and more sensible interpretation of the verse with me before I took to living in a cave and never coming out. He told me that the "fear" the verse speaks of is not that God would put his hand *on* me in some vengeful manner, but that he would take his hand *from* me and leave me to my own corrupt devices. While there's still a lot I've got to learn from the Lord, I do know enough that I don't ever want Him to remove His hand from me. I'm fearful, Lord. Lead, guide, and direct me. And let the blessings begin.

Beating Stress God's Way

In addition to the verses above, I've identified four separate principles that, if applied with heartfelt intensity, can tame the stress-monster simmering just below the surface for many of us. These principles work *every* time we put them into practice. As it is with all successful ventures, our choice of blessing over stressing all comes down to the follow-through.

Be Thankful

"Thankful? Are you kidding? Haven't you already talked enough about thankfulness in this book? Be thankful for the overtime that has no end in sight? Or the way my kids fight with each other like ninjas? Or my dropping-like-a-rock financial portfolio? Yeah … about that 'thankful thing' … I'll get back with you on that one!"

As counterintuitive as it sounds, we really are to be thankful in whatever circumstances we find ourselves. Again, Thessalonians 5:18 tells us this precisely: "Give thanks in all circumstances, for this is God's will for you in Christ Jesus." In Ephesians 5:20, we find guidelines for living a life filled with the Holy Spirit as well as the admonition to fill our days "always giving thanks

> **And we know that in all things God works for the good of those who love him, who, have been called according to his purpose.**

to God the Father for everything, in the name of our Lord Jesus Christ." Before you dismiss these charges as unreasonable and totally out of your abilities, realize this: it doesn't mean we have to like what we're going through at a particular time; it just means that we are to give thanks for wherever the Lord has placed us for the moment. We also can claim the words of Romans 8:28 that offer this comfort: "And we know that in all things God works for the good of those who love him, who, have been called according to his purpose."

I was challenged many years ago to put my faith where my mouth was when "all circumstances" and "giving thanks" wasn't the most natural response for me. Remember the beautiful red Jag I had so proudly purchased, driven to Oklahoma, and had to hose down in a run-down, out-in-the-middle-of-nowhere service station? Well, we had "Big Red" towed back home, where she remained in our detached garage as sort of an expensive reminder in humility. The car hadn't been back home for too long when my then-four-year-old son, Kyle, gave me the chance to "practice what I preach."

"Daddy! Daddy!" Kyle yelled as he raced to greet me in the driveway at the end of an especially long work day. "Daddy, come see! I washed your car for you today!"

I took his sweet, chubby little boy hand, and we headed toward the garage. Before we reached the garage, however, I was met by streams of glistening red paint coursing down the driveway and into the flower beds.

Hmmmm ... that's interesting, I thought.

Understatement. Definitely a major understatement.

We rounded the corner, and there sat my formerly beautiful, formerly shiny, formerly flawless (at least on the outside!) car. Did I mention it was a candy-apple red Jaguar XJ6? In all the earnestness of a four-year-old little boy wanting to please his daddy, Kyle had "scrubbed" the entire driver's side with a steel brush and turpentine. He was so proud he couldn't stop smiling. I was so stunned I couldn't believe my eyes. Together, we were both in complete awe of the "job" Kyle had done on my car.

"Here's where you *get* to be thankful," prompted the Holy Spirit. "Here's your son who's done the best he can do to make you proud and he's standing ready to receive your blessing." I saw the symbolism of the father-son relationship playing out right before my glazed-over eyes. This was one of those "all circumstances" I had challenged others to embrace while I stood by offering support. Now it was my turn.

It took me a minute to regain my composure, but I managed to muster up my thankfulness. I thanked my son for *his efforts,* redirected his future intentions toward his playhouse, and ultimately thanked the Lord for the perspective and the challenge to always be thankful. I recognized the car "wash" for what it was: a test. It was a test involving something I highly prized (the car) colliding with something infinitely more important (my son) and my ability to give thanks for the "collision."

I think the Lord gives us these chances to show that we're thankful *in all circumstances.* He starts with the easy ones and gradually cranks up the "difficulty" setting as we grow and mature in our relationship with Him. I told the Lord that afternoon that I might not always understand His methods, but that I was doing my best to get the concept of *all circumstances* nailed down as fast as possible! And you know the best thing that came out of the Draper "Scratch 'N Wash" experience? When

I stepped up and gave thanks for my son's well-meaning efforts, I was the one who received the blessing.

Be Prayerful

I am of the opinion that the single biggest thing we can do to reduce stress in our lives is to pray. I'm also of the opinion that the single most popular thing we *really* do is to worry. The two responses could not be more polar opposites. If you do one, it is close to impossible to do the other with any real effort. Try turning your problems over to God and seeing how effective you are at some down and dirty, gut-wrenching worrying. Maybe try it the other way: indulge in some worst-case scenario, taking your problem to its absolute worst possible resolution, and then try praying while you're doing that. See what I mean? If you're fully engaged in the one response, it just about completely precludes you from doing the other.

Now the biggest challenge we face is opting for the "praying" response rather than the "worrying" alternative. I've got to admit, it's a constant battle for me. Lots of times, without even thinking about it, I get the whole multiple choice option backward. I can be well on my way down Worry Lane when I suddenly realize, "Wait a minute, Draper, this worrying thing isn't working out quite so well for you. Let's talk about Plan B." It's usually after I've stalled out in my own efforts and worried myself sick that I'm able to call up one of the most reassuring Scriptures in the Bible. Remember Philippians 4:6–7? It says, "Do not be anxious about anything, but in everything, by prayer and petition, with thanksgiving, present your requests to God. And the peace of God, which transcends all understanding, will guard your hearts and your minds in Christ Jesus." Isn't it amazing to have a promise such as this just waiting to be claimed and yet why do we try to worry, ponder, and analyze our way through so many issues on our own? Praise God for His never-ending patience with us!

I heard recently that scientists equate one hour of worry to eight hours of hard labor. Just think if you worried only eight hours a day—

that is the equivalent to sixty-four hours of serious working! No wonder so many of us are dog-tired at the end of the day: we've spent our entire day exhausting ourselves mentally, emotionally, spiritually, and physically consumed with things we can't control. Spend too many days like this and your body will eventually voice its own objections through physical ailments that do little more than make the situation worse. Exhaustion, headaches, high blood pressure, and anxiety are some of the more minor consequences of a life that's been overtaken by unreasonable stress. Heart disease, strokes, and even death are the prize awaiting the truly committed worriers.

I almost became my own best example several years ago when I started having some troubling symptoms while on a business trip. A few days before I was to return home, my leg started swelling. It was just minor at first, and I attributed it to standing too much the previous few days. *I just need a good night's rest,* I thought at first. When the swelling had increased the following day, I tried to push it out of my mind but was mostly unsuccessful. I fought the mental battle and the physical discomfort for the next two days before it was time to head home.

I was so glad to board the plane for the flight home when I realized I was in a window seat with an elderly couple seated beside me and *between* me and the aisle. "Slow-moving" doesn't begin to describe their speed of movement! "Tough it out, Draper," I told myself as I took my seat. "It's just a two-hour flight and then you'll be home." I don't know if it was the pressurized cabin, the claustrophobic feelings that seemed to be closing in on me, or the legitimate increased swelling of both my legs, but I was about to crawl out of my skin by the time we touched down.

Because somewhere in my distant memory I seemed to remember my dad having something like this happen to him many years earlier, I called him once I was comfortably reclined on my couch. "So, dad, when this happened to you, what did the doctor think it was?" I asked.

"Well, he said it could be the beginnings of congestive heart failure," he said.

Whoa … Whoa … *Whoa!* Totally too much information! This can't be happening to *me!* I half-heartedly (no cardiac joke intended!) thanked him for the information and did the only sensible thing: I went to bed and pretended it hadn't happened and I didn't know what might possibly be the cause. So much for being an informed patient. At that moment, all I wanted was to be a weary traveler taking comfort beneath the warm and comforting covers of his own bed. And so I was. For one hour.

Little more than sixty minutes later I woke up with a startle. I was cold, clammy, lightheaded, dizzy, and having trouble catching my breath. My chest was tight and hurting, and I felt a tremor of pain going down one arm. I was freaking out physically, mentally, and emotionally.

Elizabeth rushed me to the emergency room, and after the staff took one look at my extremely elevated blood pressure, I was escorted immediately in for an examination. For the next three hours, the doctors and nurses hooked me up to monitors that measured my breaths, my pulse, and my blood pressure. They shot films of my chest, lungs, and extremities to search for blood clots and other abnormalities. At the end of my tests, the doctor overseeing my care for the evening stepped into my curtained-off corner of the room and said, "Well Mr. Draper, the good news is that you're *not* dying tonight."

The official diagnosis? Panic attack. I know, I know—how lame is that? I used to make fun of people who had panic attacks! After all, I reasoned, they had brought these "attacks" on themselves. I thought they had taken a few minor aches and pains and exploited them to the point of requiring medical attention. And yet, one sleepless night and a few thousand dollars in medical testing later and I was the proud possessor of a panic attack on my record. My "guy" friends would definitely have some fun with this!

I've since had many, many more panic attacks and would guess you have too. No, not the kind where your chest tightens up and you think you're about to faint. These kinds of panic attacks are much less invasive physically but incredibly detrimental spiritually. All it takes is for us to doubt God's infinite ability to care for us and we let worry invade our mind. With worry comes panic, and with panic comes the attack—Satan's attack. We're at our most vulnerable to Satan's panic-inducing attacks when we indulge in the destructive practice of worrying. The cure is sweet and ridiculously simple: pray. No appointment necessary. No prescription needed. Just a serious dose of time spent in the presence of Christ.

Be Thoughtful

To be thoughtful, the dictionary explains that one is marked by "careful thinking" and being "considerate of others." At first glance these definitions seem to be completely separate and not related to one another. But the closer I draw to God and the better I come to understand His purpose for His followers, the more I think the two are inextricably related. If you consider the definitions through a Christ-focused lens, it's easier to see. Whenever you have "careful thinking," believers should be led to be "considerate of others." And wherever you find believers being "considerate of others," it has probably come as the result of "careful thinking" and dwelling in the word of God.

> **Filter what you watch on television, pay for at the movies, or read in the daily newspapers against this charge.**

When it comes to our thoughts, Jesus tells us precisely what to concentrate on in Philippians 4:8: "Whatever is true, whatever is noble, whatever is right, whatever is pure, whatever is lovely, whatever is admirable—if anything is excellent or praiseworthy—think about such things." Filter what you watch on television, pay for at the movies, or read in the daily newspapers against this charge. No doubt, little of what most of us consume meets this criteria of being thoughtful.

Happy to Do It

Not surprisingly, the Bible also addresses the second half of this definition, to be "considerate of others." Words of wisdom spring from the pages of the book of Proverbs as chapter after chapter tells how to live lives of honor to the Lord and in harmony with our fellow man. One such verse, Proverbs 11:25, is brief and simple yet says volumes, "He who refreshes others will himself be refreshed." Let me give you the twenty-first-century translation: Get out of yourself! Quit dwelling on only what concerns you and do something to benefit others. Take the indulgent focus off of you and your problems and help someone worse off. They'll be blessed by your support and aid; you'll be blessed by shifting your focus off of your situation for a while.

My granddad had a saying every time I'd start complaining about not having something I thought I deserved. He used to say, "I had no shoes and complained until I met a man with no feet." Try looking beyond your immediate "crisis of the moment," to others in your church and community. I promise, being thoughtful is easier than you think.

Be Praiseful

When I think of being praiseful, I can't help but think of singing and shouting and totally cutting loose and telling others of God's glory. It's like being so utterly thankful that you can't just *speak* it, you want to shout it! You can't keep quiet about it even if you *wanted* to! This kind of nonstop, raise-the-roof, I'm-so-blessed-I-can't-stand-it praise and glory is just what Jesus wants to hear from us.

> **This kind of nonstop, raise-the-roof, I'm-so-blessed-I-can't-stand-it praise and glory is just what Jesus wants to hear from us.**

The psalmist wrote in Psalm 34:1, "I will bless the Lord at all times; his praise shall continually be in my mouth" (NASB). Don't you think this guy had a few struggles of his own? And yet he committed to praising the Lord continually—just as we are to do. Remember whatever stress has crept into your life is by God's design—either He put it there or allowed it to be there—and we are to learn from it *and* praise Him while doing so.

I heard about a woman who was suffering from chronic nightmares. Night after night, she would toss and turn as her dreams turned to nightmares, disrupting even the deepest of sleep. After a few weeks of hit-or-miss sleep, exhaustion set in and she finally made an appointment to see her doctor.

"Doctor," she said, "It's the same thing—night after night—I'm a wigwam, I'm a teepee, I'm a wigwam, I'm a teepee, I'm a …"

Immediately, the doctor pronounced his diagnosis: "Ma'am, calm down. It's clear to me: You're *two tents!*"

Okay, so that's a funny and oversimplified look at a serious ailment, but aren't we too tense most of the time? In our overbooked, overcommitted, and overextended way of life, it is all too easy to inadvertently let Stress come along for the ride. After all, we've got an extra seat at the dinner table … or room in the mini-van … or a pull-out couch in the den. But you know what I've observed about this ungracious "guest" every time he stops by? Whatever accommodations I provide, it's not enough. He wants more and more … and still more. Soon Stress has taken up residence throughout the whole house and in every member of my family. It wasn't enough just to consume me and my little corner of the house. No, once given the slightest of foothold, Stress insidiously affects and infects my thoughts, my words, and my actions. And then, as if to compound matters, it moves on to my family!

I've seen Stress hang on to bring about physical ailments, damaged relationships, and lots of mental anguish. I've learned that it's a lot like the Energizer Bunny. It keeps "going, and going, and going …" I've also learned that a deep and abiding relationship with Christ is the best defense against this unwelcome intruder. Spend a little time reading the Bible and Stress seems to start packing. Practice a lifestyle of "other-centeredness," and Stress begins to lose interest in hanging around.

Shout praises to our Heavenly Father for His gift of salvation and Stress starts looking for another home to set up shop.

It's a constant battle to keep stress at bay, but I make a conscious effort every day to keep my blessings at the forefront of my mind, and remarkably, I've found I am altogether simply "too blessed to be stressed."

For bonus content related to this chapter, please visit:
http://www.happytodoit.jlog.com

8

WHATEVER

You don't have to talk to someone too long before you're bound to hear them respond, "Whatever ..." when asked for an opinion, a choice, or a preference. Depending on the tone and the inflection used, "whatever" can take on lots of different meanings, from casual indifference ("Hey, man, whatever ... no big deal.") to insinuating insult ("Whatever, old man, you're such a loser!"). Recently, I've noticed the nonchalant attitude that "whatever" usually conveys has been taken a step further. As if enunciating the three-syllable, one-word response to all of life's big dilemmas is too taxing, teenagers have even taken to abbreviating their replies to "whatev," as in, "My dad's bummed because I totaled my car ... Whatev."

Whatev, indeed.

Most of us past our twenties use this "one-word-fits-all" response in totally innocuous ways, usually as a means of complacent agreement in lieu of a risk-taking statement of preference. These conversations usually go something along the lines of, "How about Mexican for lunch?"

"Yeah, sure ... (indignant pause). *Whatever.*"

Or what about, "Honey, let's go see that cute, romantic comedy on Saturday night ... Honey?"

Happy to Do It

"Sure, darling, whatever."

See how we use this compound word to say one thing but in all likelihood, mean something entirely different? It's not like you're trying to be unusually contentious or overtly disagreeable when you drop the "W" bomb, but you're also not offering up genuine, enthusiastic support either. It's kind of like taking the often-traveled "path of least resistance" verbally but inwardly allowing thoughts and feelings of disinterest, resentment, and disrespect to go unaddressed. It all comes down to the attitude with which we say *"whatever."* That does the real communicating to others.

"Sure, God ... Whatever!"

Sadly, many Christ-followers develop a *"whatever"* attitude toward God at the first sign of challenge in their Christian walk. Life can be moving along smoothly and then we meet up with cantankerous co-workers, disagreeable spouses, or belligerent children, and before long, we're seeing every relationship, every challenge, or everything that doesn't go just our way with a, *"Whatever ... God"* mind-set. Instead of seeing the opportunities within these challenges, we take the easy way out and develop a "come what may," resigned, and complacent perspective to what could otherwise be some of life's most enriching relationships and experiences.

I've come to realize that, if we are really intent on living lives reflective of Christ's love within us, then it follows that we need to speak and act as Jesus would if He were to face our specific situations. You know the kind of situations I'm talking about—those situations involving the endless challenges that dealing with others frequently presents—challenges such as disrespect, envy, strife, anxiety, and insecurity that oftentimes manifest themselves through hurtful words, ulterior motives, and deceitful actions. Jesus dealt with all these anger issues and many more during His years on Earth, and yet He did so through righteous confrontation, straightforward words, and the extension of grace and mercy to those least deserving in the eyes of the world.

First "Who," Then "What"

Before we can even begin to address our issues with others, we've got to first pay close attention to the "who" Christ would have us be. We have to become like Christ and become *"whoever"* He designed us to be. As the Bible tells us in John 3:16, the reward for being a *"whoever"* in Christ is the promise of an eternity of God's blessings: "For God so loved the world, that He gave His one and only Son, that *whoever* believes in Him shall not perish but have eternal life." (NASB) God clearly lays it out for all of us considering adoption into His family. He wants his followers to become the *who* He designed them to be before we consider tackling the *whatever* He would have us do.

One of the most well-read business authors in the last decade is Jim Collins, author of *Built to Last* and *Good to Great.* Through his lengthy research of corporate best practices, review of mountains of statistical data, and many, many hours of personal interviewing, Collins has garnered some keen observations and insightful perspective into

> **For God so loved the world, that He gave His one and only Son, that whoever believes in Him shall not perish but have eternal life.**

the men and women who run some of the country's most successful companies. Foremost among his findings is that the top fifty companies within the Fortune 500 are particularly adept at addressing the "first *who*, then *what*" issue before tackling the outside forces of their respective industry's marketplace. As Collins puts it, "You've got to get the right people on the bus" before you can go anywhere.

I heard Mr. Collins in person at an industry meeting, and he held my interest like few speakers have in recent memory. This guy really knows what he is talking about. In presenting some of his findings from his research about what makes companies not just successful but *super*-successful, he said, "As I've been studying these companies, I've discovered something … and what I've discovered is that these companies had a philosophy of 'first *who*, then *what*.'" As he spoke these words, I couldn't help but think that's how it is with God and His plans for our lives. He tells us He's got some "whatevers" that He wants us to be involved in, but before we can take them on, we've got to become the "whoever" it is He wants us to be. Anything short of this diminishes our potential for affecting Christ's Kingdom.

So What's the "What"?

Because I'm generally a "glass half full" kind of guy, I'm going to assume you're feeling completely convicted about living a life worthy of Christ's honor. You're regularly conscious of Christ's unfathomable gift of eternal life and at least most of the time, are intentional in your actions and words to live accordingly. Now begins the journey to tackle—no, make that "the journey to *embrace*"—as you encounter the *whatevers* Christ allows to come your way.

First, however, I want you to completely understand just how broad of a brushstroke this *"whatever"* thing is that we've casually come to pepper our everyday conversation with. You see, whenever we drop a nonchalant "whatever," what we're really saying is "anything or everything,"[1] according to the dictionary. Brief, but oh-so-complete. Read it again … I'll wait.

"A-N-Y-T-H-I-N-G and … E-V-E-R-Y-T-H-I-N-G."

Take a moment and let that sink in. Totally overwhelmed yet? Give it time. You will be as you come to the sobering realization that following Christ doesn't leave much out, does it? Actually, it doesn't leave *any*thing or *any*one out. From the Lord's perspective, when we become one of His *whoevers*, we're committing to all the *whatevers* He allows across our path.

No "What about *this* person?"

Or "How 'bout *that* situation?"

Or even a "You gotta be kidding!"

Think about this definition next time you're tempted to throw out a casual and noncommittal "*whatever*."

Picture a husband asking his wife about the evening's plans: "Hey honey, want to go to the game tonight?"

"Anything or everything, dear."

Huh? Is that a yes or a no? Does she mean "anything" *but* go to the game? Or "anything" is okay? Maybe she even means that she's good with "everything" going to the game entails and then some!? See what I mean? Not only does the word "*whatever*" not accurately reflect our intentions, but the ambiguity is oftentimes intentional! We don't want to go "on the record" as stating preference or offering an alternative, but we also don't want to be cornered into being accountable for taking a stand.

If we're honest with ourselves, all of us take on this weak-willed, compliance-by-default attitude with Christ at one time or another. Maybe once a week. Maybe once a day. Maybe ten times before noon! However frequently we adopt this attitude of neglect, it's too much.

Actions, Words, Thoughts, and Possessions

Actions

Consider how radically different our actions, words, and thoughts would be if we were *intentional* in our use of "*whatever*" as we worked to live out Christ's example for us. Consider the admonition of 1 Corinthians 10:31 as it tells us, "So whether you eat or drink or *whatever* you do, do it all for the glory of God."

Now sub in our literal definition: "So whether you eat or drink or *anything and everything* you do, do it all for the glory of God." Incredible, isn't it? Paul is telling us that, as an act of reverence and a heart overflowing with gratitude for our very salvation, we are to do *anything and everything* for the glory of God. Even the simplest of acts, such as eating and drinking, are to be done in such a manner as to bring glory to God.

When I first honestly considered that even something as ordinary as eating and drinking could glorify the Lord, it was a tough bit to swallow—literally! I'm the kind of guy who loves food from each of the four food groups—fast, frozen, instant, and chocolate! I'm also the guy who, when my buddies gave me a hard time about getting into shape, replied, "I *am* in shape! The shape I picked is a *triangle*." On top of that, I'm also the quick-witted husband who rebuffed my wife's carb-counting comments when I reached for another piece of bread by telling her, "Jesus is *the* bread of life. I'm just trying to fill up on holiness!"

Seriously, though, I know that if I were to totally embrace this challenge, I'd think longer and harder before polishing off that bag of chips while watching a football game. Are those extra calories and fat grams *really* going to improve my witness? Will super-sizing my "burger deal" bring joy to others? And my personal favorite—will ordering a Diet Coke with my cheese fries cause others to rejoice at my restraint?

> **The bigger issue is for me and you to grasp the endless opportunities we all encounter on a daily basis to act for the glory of God.**

Though I make light (or is it lite?!) of my frequent food dilemmas, the bigger issue is for me and you to grasp the endless opportunities we all encounter on a daily basis to act for the glory of God. Wherever we find ourselves in—the boardroom, the classroom, the grocery store, and beyond—we have within us the privilege of acting on behalf of the glorious grace that has been extended to us through life in Christ.

Consider how this could impact your co-workers and other business associates.

Realize the influence you could extend to troubled family members and friends.

Dare to intentionally live the life of one who's been saved by grace for all the world to see, and prepare to be used by God in unimaginable ways!

Words

Just like our actions, our words also have an amazing potential for fulfilling the "anything and everything" that God would have each of us to do. Colossians 3:17 reinforces this challenge to speak as one filled with Christ's love: "And *whatever* you do, whether in word or deed, do it all in the name of the Lord Jesus, giving thanks to God the Father through him." For the sake of making my point once again about all that "*whatever*" encompasses regarding the Lord, read the verse again with the dictionary definition substituted in. "And *anything and everything* you do, whether in word or deed, do it all in the name of the Lord Jesus, giving thanks to God the Father through him." *Anything and everything* I say should be honor to the Father? Makes me think of Ricky Ricardo's famous line to Lucy after one of her infamous fiascos: "Lucy … you got some 'splainin' to do!"

Lord, I've got some 'splainin' to do, too. Lots of it …

One of my more colorful memories of a time before conviction regarding my words had taken a hold of my life was on my fifteenth birthday. We were living in Del City, Oklahoma and my dad was the pastor at First Southern Baptist Church. Some members of the youth group and a couple of the youth pastors were going all out for this birthday, and I was pumped!

Besides inviting upward of one hundred of my "closest friends," I had taken the liberty of inviting my then-girlfriend who lived on the other side of the city. Though she'd met my friends a few times before, there was something about her that just didn't sit well with my group. I never really knew what it was, but thought I'd make a point that night and invited her just to show them who was in charge.

As the night wore on, so did the off-handed comments about my girlfriend. I picked up bits of conversation as I mingled around the patio. At one point, I could even see my friends huddled together, talking and laughing about this girl I had brought to my party. With every chuckle from the group across the room, I grew more and more angry. I could feel the heat rising in my cheeks by the minute and my heartbeat reverberating in my eardrums.

As if this critical review of my girlfriend by my so-called friends wasn't sufficient to send me into teenage, anger-infused orbit, one of the guys thought it would be fun to toss the birthday boy into the pool as a joke.

Bad idea, dude.

Totally bad idea.

I couldn't have been in the pool longer than three seconds. No sooner had my feet hit the bottom than I shot out of the pool and smack in the middle of my snickering and equally "mature" friends. The only difference between us, however, was that they kept their judgmental and colorful comments amongst themselves. Regrettably, that was not the case with "yours truly."

I was dripping wet and *in their faces*, words flying and water flinging. When I say I was "in their faces," believe me—I was in their faces! Not only was I yelling and hollering, but I was also cussing like a sailor. I said all the four-letter words I knew and circled back around in case I left one unsaid the first time through!

Needless to say, my outburst of colorful vocabulary was a showstopper. Everybody from the deacons to the dog heard the pastor's son cut loose with a string of expletives completely unfitting of one who claimed to be a Christ-follower. It definitely wasn't one of my proudest moments, but it eventually came to be a tremendous learning opportunity and undoubtedly the most gracious gift I received for my birthday that year.

It wasn't long after that incident that I came to fully appreciate just what the apostle Matthew meant when he said, "For *whatever* is in your heart determines what you say" (Matthew 12:34, NLT). Again, let us replace *whatever* with its literal definition: "For *anything and everything* that is in your heart determines what you say." That means that whenever you're reduced to gut-level reactions (say, for example, being thrown in a pool!) and without the benefit of forethought to measure your words, what springs forth and spills from your mouth is a true reflection of what fills your heart. Is it just me, or is it getting hot in here?

Think of your heart as the fountain or the source within you and the words that come forth as the stream. Better yet, picture this old, rusty water spigot like the one I came across on a hunting trip many years ago. It was just outside a dilapidated cabin set deep in the woods that had long since been abandoned. My hunting buddies and I thought we'd see if there was still water running through the line, and so one of the guys twisted the metal knob a full 360° before anything happened. A few labored gurgles and lots of spitting and sputtering later and out came a rush of the muddiest, dirtiest, foulest-smelling water you have ever seen or smelled. Not only was it vile and disgusting, but it came with such force and so quickly that it splattered all over those of us standing around it.

> **Whatever fills the source is what spews forth.**

See the correlation?

Whatever fills the source is what spews forth. Maybe not today. Maybe not when all the plates are spinning. But eventually, when circumstances are not to our liking or completely within our control, what is within will surface. Plan ahead. Fill your fountain and temper your source with Christ's love, because the alternative can be devastating to you and those around you.

A word of instruction to those of you contemplating cleaning out your "fountain"—by all means, clean it out! Scrub, scour, and clean until nothing dishonoring remains, but be just as intentional to fill it with words of praise, songs of thanksgiving, and prayers of glory, because if you fail to fill the vacancy, it's just a matter of time before the old and ingrained habits of the past will rush in to fill the void.

Jesus warned us of this danger when He spoke of the man from whom He had earlier cast out a demon. When the man did nothing to fill the emptiness left by the demon, the man became vulnerable to *whatever*—that is *anything and everything*—that posed a threat. When the once-removed demon realized his former "residence" had remained empty, he quickly collected seven of his friends and the eight demons returned and filled the man, making him much worse off than before the first one ever left him. Learn from his example: a heart void of love and adoration for Christ is fair game for *anything and everything* to take up residence within. Immerse yourself in Christ's words through a regular Bible study and hang out the "No Vacancy" sign on your heart permanently.

I saw a billboard on my way to the Milwaukee airport that spoke to the heart of speaking our heart. It said, "If you must swear, use your own name. – God." I chuckled at first, and then I got to thinking about it.

"Randy, dammit." Doesn't sound quite right, does it?

Okay, maybe it just sounds funny to me because that's my name. Let me try my barber's name, John. "John, dammit." Still doesn't sound right.

Maybe I should try that with Elizabeth's name … "Elizabeth..." Nah, not such a good idea (I can just imagine all the guys nodding in agreement with me!).

I think you're smart enough to see where this is going and realize that, because we've conditioned ourselves to hearing and/or speaking God's name alongside of this word intended to call down damnation from Heaven that we're used to it and unphased by what it's actually saying and generally accepting of the two-word plea for damnation. Did you catch that? Look at it this way: by thinking, speaking, or muttering "God, dammit," you are literally asking God not to exercise His endless potential to bless you beyond measure and instead, to damn you and *whatever* (read: *anything and everything*) it is you're trying to accomplish. That's counter-productivity of an eternal sort and one pitfall within our power to avoid at all costs.

Thoughts

By now you may be thinking, "Hey, isn't it enough that, by my words and my actions, I'm pursuing this life of Christ? Can't I at least entertain a few 'get even' schemes in my mind or maybe imagine a particularly colorful conversation I'd like to have with my boss were my paycheck not dependent upon it?" Not going to happen, friend. Not going to happen.

Just as the Bible gives us clear direction regarding our words and our actions, it also addresses what is frequently the last frontier we surrender to Christ: our thoughts. Philippians 4:7–8 gives us a "laundry list" of sorts about where we are to focus our thoughts: "Brothers, *whatever* is true, *whatever* is noble, *whatever* is right, *whatever* is pure, *whatever* is lovely, *whatever* is admirable—if anything is excellent or praiseworthy—think about such things."

So you know what's coming next ... let's once again replace *whatever* with its definition: "Brothers, *anything and everything* that is true, *anything and everything* that is noble, *anything and everything* that is right, *anything and everything* that is pure, *anything and everything* that is lovely, *anything and everything* that is admirable—if anything is excellent or praiseworthy—think about such things." Isn't it amazing how the magnitude of this verse increases ten-fold just by replacing the word with its definition?

Try applying this litmus test of honor to the movies you watch at home, in the theater, or in the hotel on "pay-per-view." Think of these boundaries in regard to the sites you surf on the Internet or the chat rooms you frequent. Consider these guidelines against the books, newspapers, and magazines you read. Would *anything and everything* you allow to fill your mind and consume your thoughts be considered true, noble, and right? Could you identify it as pure, lovely, and admirable? If not, it may be time to take stock of what influences you allow to infiltrate your mind and thought processes.

Chances are, whatever it is you watch, surf, or read are not egregiously offensive. I've got to confess that I used to watch any and every Sylvester

Stallone or Arnold Swartzenegger movie that came out. "These blow 'em up, shoot 'em up movies don't affect me," I told myself. "After all, they're shot on a Hollywood sound stage with fake guns and gallons of fake blood." Yeah, I knew they were all nothing more than carefully orchestrated explosions and extremely coordinated chase scenes, and yet, I found myself living a fearful life.

I came face to face with these fears one evening during a prayer meeting when I asked God why I was living so fearfully. Conviction about the violent movies I was so frequently watching came to mind. I hadn't even realized that, bit by bit, these movies were affecting my everyday life—to the point where I was more than just a little bit jumpy when I took the trash out to the curb. It's humorous now, but more than once I half-expected someone to jump out from behind the

> **For most of us, it's the subtle outside influences that have the biggest impact on our thoughts and perspectives.**

bushes and nail me with a laser beam to the chest! My solution: cease and desist on the over-the-top, killing spree kind of movies. Now I've taken to watching romantic comedies with my wife. She's happy for the company, and I all but skip when I'm taking out the trash!

For most of us, it's the subtle outside influences that have the biggest impact on our thoughts and perspectives. Maybe it's a casually presented scene in a movie or a possibly suggestive/possibly innocent comment from a friend on a social networking site or even the liberally slanted presentation of the nightly local newscast that creeps into our consciousness and alters our perception of what is truly good. Oftentimes these seemingly benign outside influences insidiously infiltrate and adjust our boundaries of right and wrong. The problem is that for the overwhelming majority of them, these influences are not measured against the Bible's directives, but against pop culture's constantly changing level of acceptable behavior.

Possessions

The pastor of my home church, Fellowship Church, is Ed Young and he has a way of cutting through whatever excuse you throw his way when it comes to living our lives as a testimony for Christ's unfailing love. One area he's particularly intent on helping folks in is in regard to seeing the temporal value of their possessions. As an accomplished wordsmith, Ed has even given a name to all the symbols, signs, and representations of material wealth. Be it a fifty-two-inch plasma, a diamond tennis bracelet, or a top-of-the-line skateboard, Ed simply calls it all "bling, bling, ca-ching, ca-ching."

And while Ed's catchy nickname for all things purchased and possessed is clever and memorable, it's most important to realize that Christ's intent for all that we possess is to be used to share His love with others. Any other use is selfish and dishonorable to the Lord. The apostle Paul knew and practiced this belief better than anyone in the Bible. He'd had a lot, lost a lot, and been everywhere "in between," but since the point of his conversion from a Christ-doubter to a Christ-follower, he exemplified the "can't take it with you" philosophy like no one else of his time.

In the book of Philippians, Paul takes a retrospective view of his life before coming to believe in Christ. He speaks of his family's honorable lineage, his respected position in society, and even his perfect track record regarding his persecution of believers. However, upon receiving the Spirit of the Lord on the road to Damascus, all this accomplishment, societal rank, and the material wealth that he possessed were for naught …totally useless…wasted effort. In his challenge to the believers in Philippi, he told all who would listen, "But whatever was to my profit I now consider loss for the sake of Christ. What is more, I consider everything a loss compared to the surpassing greatness of knowing Christ Jesus my Lord, for whose sake I have lost all things. I consider them rubbish, that I may gain Christ and be found in him …" (Philippians 3:7–9a).

Did you catch the beginning of the verse? Paul said, "*Whatever* was to my profit I now consider loss." Now read it this way: "*anything and everything* I now consider loss for the sake of Christ." Could you say the same thing about all your possessions? Your place in office hierarchy? Your standing within your community or church? Consider whatever it is that you consider to be of most earthly value and ask yourself, "Has my attainment of this possession, this title, or this reputation come at the price of knowing and living for Christ?" If you answered yes, you undoubtedly overpaid—and in much more than dollars and cents. The good news, though, is that Christ's currency of love, grace, mercy, and forgiveness is sufficient to buy back all of our costly "possessions" in exchange for acceptance of His love.

Keep this tremendous "rate of exchange" in mind the next time you purchase a bigger, flatter television or another so-called time-saving gadget or one more "to-die-for" pair of shoes and ask yourself, "Do I have things or do things have *me*?" If what you're buying or what you're seeking compromises what you live for in terms of your identity in Christ, it's not worth the price.

I heard about a wealthy fellow who didn't quite get this concept and was intent on taking his earthly wealth with him beyond the grave. So intent was the man that he directed his wife to bury him with all his money when the time came. Ever the dutiful wife, she agreed, and the man lived out the rest of his days content in the knowledge that his money would follow him to his grave.

Upon the man's death, the funeral was held, and the grieving widow cried quietly on the front row during the service. At the pastor's invitation to pay her final respects, the widow stepped toward the open casket, placed a small box beside the man's hand, and sweetly kissed his cheek. Graveside services followed, and then the final interment.

As the crowd dispersed at the cemetery, caretakers began lowering the casket into the grave as the new widow made her way back to the limousine. Now, because her best friend had known of the husband's money arrangement and had witnessed her friend deposit the box in the casket at the church, she watched from afar as shovelful after shovelful filled the deep, deep hole.

Incredulously, the friend bolted for the limo and grabbed her friend. "Barbara, Barbara! I know you're distraught, but did you really bury Jerry with all his money in that little box?"

"Well, yes, I did honor his wishes," the widow replied. "I wrote him a check for all of it. If he can cash it, he can have it!"

Though clever and funny, this story is a great illustration of the fact that we can't take anything of the earth with us when we die, but we can certainly send it ahead by building treasure in Heaven through our relationships on earth and by coming to the point where we willingly and joyfully commit all that we have and all that we'll ever have to Christ. The treasures of Heaven are ours to build, and the Lord has given us all the tools we need to construct mansions beyond imagination. The tools of the trade for constructing a Christ-honoring life are found in the *whatevers* of our daily lives in our actions, words, thoughts, and possessions.

God's "Whatever" Is Not "Whenever"

Have you ever known someone who lives by the saying, "If it wasn't for the last minute, nothing would get done"? Maybe it's you or your spouse or your kids. It's like you (or they) know something's got to be done, but until it's crunch time (and by that I mean a boss breathing down your neck, a parent hollering at a kid, or a "minor" holiday like Christmas looming ahead), you don't act. You've got plenty of time, you tell yourself. That is if the computer doesn't freeze. Or the teacher extends the due date for the book reports. Or you're planning on buying your gifts from Walgreen's clearance aisle for Christmas.

Putting off and perpetually procrastinating our individual responsibilities, be they at home, work, school, or otherwise, is a personal decision, as are the consequences for incomplete and unsatisfactory performance. The option to be the whoever for Christ in *whatever* capacity *whenever* He would have us serve are not ours to negotiate, delay, or decide. Deuteronomy 12:32 expressly tells of our responsibility to act *whenever* called upon to do God's work: *"Whatever* I command you, you shalt be careful to do. You should not add to nor take away from it"* (NASB).

The good news is that the *whenevers* that God would have us be His light are at literally every juncture of our days and nights, for it is *whenever* we are with others that we have the opportunity to speak hope into their lives. It's our responsibility, however, to recognize and embrace these situations *whenever* God presents them to us and to act accordingly, not *whenever* it is convenient for us.

People who only act *whenever* it is convenient for them remind me of couples who say they are waiting until they have enough money to raise a child before starting their family. Not to discount financial responsibility in the least, but if you're waiting until you have enough to cover everything raising a child entails, you run the risk of never having enough and missing the opportunity entirely. The same principle holds true exponentially for acting whenever the Holy Spirit presents a chance to be the light of Jesus to others: wait too long and the moment passes ... forever.

If convenience is the measurement by which we live for Christ, then it's a guarantee that other distractions will undoubtedly interfere and/ or take precedence. When that happens, the *whenever* to be a *whoever* and to do *whatever* comes and goes and the chance to live unto Christ in that moment is forever lost.

Sobering?

Convicting?

Hopefully.

God's "Whatever" Is "Wherever"

You are game to become *whoever* Christ would have you to be. You're "on" to do whatever Christ asks *whenever* He asks. And now, the final piece to the "sold-out for Christ" persona—you gotta do all this *wherever* Christ places you to minister—not just the planned-for two hours at the soup kitchen with your Sunday school class or with the clerk at the Goodwill Store when you drop off your discards or when you drop a dollar in the red kettle on your way into the mall.

Because, as the old saying goes, "Everybody is *somewhere*," our call to be the light *wherever* we are is totally and completely all encompassing. Sometimes this is easily doable. Other times … not so much. Ease of execution, you'll note, is not one of the contributing factors to living for Christ.

> ## "Ease of execution, you'll note, is not one of the contributing factors to living for Christ."

Joseph was a young man who knew the importance of serving God *wherever* he found himself. As the youngest of twelve sons, he was clearly his father's favorite. As the preference increased, so also did the resentment among his older brothers to the point where they devised a plan to take Joseph off by himself and leave him to die in a deep pit. Overcome by a twinge of conscience at the last minute, the brothers decide to sell their brother into slavery instead of a certain death.

As a slave in the house of Potiphar, Joseph is seduced by Potiphar's wife. When he rebuffs her advances, his master's wife turns the tables and accuses Joseph of being the one who made the advances. This results in a lengthy jail sentence for the innocent young man but not an absence of ministry opportunities. As Joseph serves out his sentence, his testimony of belief in God's provision for him does not go without notice. Because the Lord was with Joseph and He extended His kindness to him, Joseph found favor in the sight of the chief jailer. As a result, the chief jailer committed the care of all the prisoners to Joseph's care and did so without any supervision because, as Genesis 39:23 says, "The Lord was with Joseph and gave him success at whatever he did."

Think about all Joseph endured—abandonment and betrayal by his own brothers, a life of slavery, malicious and false accusations by his master's wife—and yet through it all, he held fast to his belief in the Lord's provision for his life and honored the Lord through his words and actions *wherever* the trickery of others landed him. When I consider the challenge to be like Christ *wherever* I am and the circumstances are of my own making, it makes Joseph's testimony to serve *wherever* that much more honorable.

Putting It All Together

Let me encourage you to remember that this journey toward holiness is a gradual process and to remember it is the first, and most critical, step in the trek. It is imperative to keep in mind that, before any of the *whatevers*, *whenevers*, and *wherevers* of life can be tackled, becoming a *whoever* for Christ is the first and foremost honorable action we can take. Don't overlook this vital first step, and don't rush the process. Don't discount Christ's ability to forgive and forget your sins of the past and think you'll skip the becoming part of this equation and move on to the action part of the plan. It doesn't work that way. Without the commitment to become a *whoever* for Christ, the other actions are simply reduced to goodwill toward your fellow man or courteous displays of kindness. And while these are admirable traits, without the motivation to honor Christ in all that you do and say and think and have, they're diluted immeasurably.

Consider the impact one person—you—could have if you were to first become *whoever* God would have you to become. Then, guided and inspired by the Holy Spirit, what if you were to greet each and every day and every personal encounter with the attitude to do *whatever* Christ would have you do *whenever* He would have you do it and *wherever* He would have you do it.

One person.

Impacting everyone he/she came in contact with in a single day.

Day after day.

Person after person.

Then consider the effect if two were to practice the *whoever/ whatever/ whenever/wherever* commandments of the Father.

Or a life group.

Or an entire church.

Heaven's population is increased by one sin-filled, Christ-searching soul at a time. If you haven't reserved your place in eternity with Christ, accept the invitation and become the glorious *whoever* Christ has designed you to be. If your eternal "reservations" are secure, first *rejoice!*—and then get about the business of living out your gratitude through *whatever* you do, *whenever* you do it, and *wherever* you go. The mansions of Heaven are filled with saints who have gone on before us, but rest assured, there's always room for *anyone and everyone* who calls upon the name of Jesus—*whoever* you are, *whatever* you've done, *whenever* you call, and *wherever* you are in life.

Just say, "Happy to do it" to Christ and let Him use you to glorify your Heavenly Father through the "*whatevers*" of your life. You will be blessed, and God will use you to be a blessing in the lives of others. One simple statement is all it takes: "*Lord, whatever you ask, I will be happy to do it!*"

For bonus content related to this chapter, please visit:
http://www.happytodoit.jlog.com

1Merriam-Webster. "whatever." Merriam-Webster.com. http://merriam-webster. com/dictionary/whatever (accessed August 16, 2010).

EPILOGUE

"I'm starting with the man in the mirror;
I'm asking him to change his ways;
No message could have been any clearer...
if you wanna make the world a better place,
take a look at yourself, and then make a change..."

Who could imagine?

I mean, really...who would have ever thought that some of the most prophetic words ever to be spoken were originally woven into a #1 pop song recorded by a skinny, high-pitched kid from Detroit who became famous for his incredible song-writing skills, on-stage gyrations, wearing only one sequined glove, and who ultimately went on to become known as 'the King of Pop.'

Michael Jackson was one of the most (if not THE most!) accomplished performers of all time, and I've got to give him credit for realizing where true change—change for the better—must begin...

With me.

With you.

With anyone intent on leaving this spinning blue marble we call 'home' a better place for their having been on it.

I know I'm not alone in my hopes…make that passionate hopes that the world will be even the slightest bit better off for my brief stay here. You want it, too…you know you do. So does your spouse. And your family. And your friends. I mean, do you really know anyone who doesn't want their life to count for something? Who doesn't want to be remembered as making a difference in at least a few lives? Who doesn't want to 'leave their mark?'

> **At the end of our lives, many of us experience a terminal case of the 'what ifs,' the 'if onlys,' and the 'woulda, coulda, shouldas.'**

I think what it all boils down to is that most of us are 'sick & tired' of being 'sick & tired' with simply getting through the day or the week or the deadline or a particular phase of our lives. We're living for Friday; trying to hang on until pay day; or hoping to make it through the holidays. We spend our days stretching our physical, emotional, spiritual, and financial resources pursuing things that won't contribute even the slightest to 'makin' the world a better place.' And regrettably we find that, at the end of our lives, many of us experience a terminal case of the 'what ifs,' the 'if onlys,' and the 'woulda, coulda, shouldas.'

It doesn't have to be this way. Let my encouragement to you and your belief in Jesus Christ be supernaturally transformed by His unimaginable powers. Let this be the starting point to put into practice some of the Christ-based principles in the preceding chapters and the beginning of a new way of living. I'm not talking about an overnight personality transplant but rather a gradual and steady process of trial and error, a learning and re-learning of important life lessons, and a growing from the experiences along the way.

Imagine a director giving you your cue to begin from this day forward to live for Christ. You hear the snap of the clapboard and receive (I mean really receive!) instructions to take the first scene in this production called

"Your Life." **"Lights, Camera, Action!"** the director barks and suddenly the camera is rolling and recording every word you speak, every action you take, every expression you show.

You're only a few days into this production when you abruptly realize this ain't no Disney cartoon. This motion picture is an action film—a high-impact, hanging-from-the-cliff-by-your-fingernails kind of action flick that comes complete with special effects beyond your imagination! But, hang on, because with a little **Weight Training**, you'll be able to carry the scene and perform all your own stunts—quite impressive for someone previously unaccustomed to maintaining much **A-Count-Ability,** but who has come to realize that they are simply **Too Blessed to be Stressed—Whatever** the scene calls for!

Amazing, isn't it, how terrific life can be when you gather a bit of momentum and you're challenged to do more simply because you're filled with Christ's abundant love? Soon you're rubbing off on the other actors in the scene, extending kindness for flubbed lines, forgotten cues, and mechanical mishaps. It's almost as if you're giving off a sort of **Radar Love** to everyone you associate with in scene after scene. It isn't long before others want to experience this comforting calm about you, a kindness and serenity that almost defies explanation as you continually show **Thanks Giving** regardless of your circumstances.

You go through scene after scene. Some you star in; others you just play a supporting role; and still others are nothing more than a cameo appearance. Before long—much sooner than you realized—you hear the final snap of the scene clapper and the director yells, "Cut! It's a wrap! Nice job, everyone."

The sets are struck, the lights are dimmed, and you exit the stage. The reviews are exceptional and you hear the words that every Christ-follower longs to ultimately hear, "Well done, my good and faithful servant..." to which you gratefully and humbly reply... **"Happy to Do It**, Lord...so very, very **Happy to Do It!"**

So now it's up to you. You have the choice. Will you be *Hacked to Do It* or *Happy to Do It?* My prayer is that you will **Get Your 'Snap' On** and be unbelievably '**Happy to Do It!**'

Happy to Do It

GET YOUR 'SNAP' ON!

"Have this attitude in yourselves which was also in Christ Jesus..."

– Philippians 2:5